personal
decision points

Compliments of

HM **Hanson McClain®**
Independent Investment Advice

personal
decision points
7 STEPS TO YOUR IDEAL RETIREMENT TRANSITION

SCOTT HANSON

IRISH
CANON
PRESS

2625 ALCATRAZ AVENUE, SUITE 105
BERKELEY CA 94705

© 2016 by Scott Hanson

Cover design: Michele Wetherbee (michelewetherbee.com)
Interior design: Design Corps (designcorps.us)

Name: Hanson, Scott.
Title: *Personal Decision Points : 7 Steps to Your Ideal
    Retirement Transition* / Scott Hanson.
Description: Berkeley [California]: Irish Canon Press, 2016.
Identifiers: ISBN 978-0-9898754-5-5
Subjects: LCSH Finance, Personal. | Retirement income--Planning. |
    Retirement--Planning. | BISAC BUSINESS & ECONOMICS /
    Personal Finance / Retirement Planning.
Classification: LCC HG179 .H268 2016 | DDC 332.024/014--dc23.

We hope you enjoy this book from **Irish Canon Press.**

Irish Canon Press
2625 Alcatraz Avenue, Suite 105
Berkeley, CA 94705

1 3 5 7 9 10 8 6 4 2

Printed in the United States of America

CONTENTS

THIS BOOK IS
DEDICATED
WITH LOVE
TO MY LATE
MOTHER-IN-LAW,
BETTY HYLTON,
WHO LIVED
RETIREMENT WELL.

RETIREMENT INCOME NEEDS

IN THIS CHAPTER
YOU WILL LEARN...

- *How to determine your retirement income needs*

- *It's not about how much money you have, it's what you do with it*

- *About the uncertain future of Social Security*

If You're **UNPREPARED**,
Facing the Retirement
Abyss Is Scary

Here's a retirement transition story that's sadly common: I recently had an appointment with a 62-year-old man named Bill who had just lost his job. Earlier that week his supervisor had walked into his office and informed him that his position was being eliminated.

Bill and his wife Sue had spent their entire careers with the same company (it's actually where they'd met), and between them had accumulated over $1 million in their 401(k)s. Yet even though they'd had the foresight to spend decades socking money away for the future, they'd never before met with an advisor because both assumed that the end was years away.

Unfortunately, the loss of Bill's job wasn't their only dilemma. At 62, maybe he could find something else, maybe he couldn't. The biggest blow to their hopes of a smooth retirement transition had actually taken place a few weeks earlier, when a serious (though manageable) illness had forced Sue to retire.

While distressing, forced retirements like these are extremely common. According to an AARP study published in the June 3rd, 2015, edition of *USA Today*, due to health issues, the health of a loved one, or the loss of a job, about 55 percent of people are forced to retire earlier than they planned.

Sitting at the table with Bill and Sue, I could see from the looks on their faces that their emotions ran the gamut from hope to anxiety and fear.

As happens during appointments, you can't help but get emotionally involved. I remember thinking how much I wanted to be able to help them.

I set about trying to better understand their situation. I asked if they had any other assets beside their retirement accounts, and they both quietly told me no. I then wrote the amount of their 401(k)s down on a piece of paper in bold, black ink, and circled it.

"Now all we have to do is make sure this money lasts you for the rest of your lives," I said.

Bill's expression dropped. My comment had taken him completely by surprise.

After what seemed like an eternity, he laughed nervously and asked, "Do we have enough?"

I remember wondering that exact same thing.

The next thing we did was to create a budget. Bill and Sue listed the things they *hoped* to do, such as fishing, college courses, a golf club membership, and some travel. Then they listed the things they wouldn't live without, such as staying in their current home.

I went to work determining a reasonable rate of return on the $1 million, subtracted fixed and discretionary expenses (their mortgage, outstanding debt, and Sue's special healthcare needs alone added up to more than $7,300 a month), and then I added in options for taking Social Security now, or waiting until later.

Then something unpleasant happened. Sitting across from Bill and Sue, two hardworking people who deserved better, I had to look them in the eye and tell them that their $1 million wasn't going to last them 10 years.

I hated seeing the look of disappointment on their faces. Especially because I knew then, as I do now, that if they'd only started planning earlier—perhaps if they had come to see me as little as three years before—their disappointment might have been avoided.

Then Sue, who had mostly been quiet throughout the meeting, asked me something that I like to refer to as "The Question of Questions." In fact, in my more than two decades as an investment advisor, this is the single most common question that I've been asked.

Sue asked, "Scott, how much money *does* it take to retire?"

How It Works in
Our **REAL** World

If you've been proactive and saved and planned for retirement, you should be proud. Simply, where there's preparation, there are options.

But all too often, people save a certain amount of money, millions even, and then they think, "I've done the work, and now it's time to live it up!"

Living off your savings may mean that you're able to meet your needs for a while, but a few health emergencies, along with ordinary day-by-day depletion, mean that, even with Social Security, you can still run out of money.

Unfortunately, the too-fast depletion of retirement savings is something I see all the time. In fact, according to an exhaustive 2014 AARP report titled "Boomers and the Great Recession," 60 percent of the people *who have saved for retirement* still run out of money a full 9 years before they die.

Obviously, the risk of running out of money is real. And, perhaps not so obviously, on its own, $700,000, $1 million, or even $2 million in savings does not guarantee you'll have enough money to last you for the rest of your life.

40%
(will have enough)

60%
(will run out of money)

RETIREES
(who have saved for retirement)

The Question
EVERYONE Asks

While I often hear the "How much money do I need to retire?" question in first-time appointments, it's even more likely to be posed to me by callers to our weekly radio show, *Hanson McClain's Money Matters*, which I've co-hosted for 20 years with my business partner, Pat McClain.

The question "How much money do I need to retire?" makes perfect sense. It's human nature to want a finite answer to wrap our heads around and to help us prepare.

Yet while that question may make sense, it's unanswerable unless I've been able to do the groundwork for that particular individual. It's unanswerable because *not only* does everyone have different hopes and dreams, but over the course of our lives, our wants, needs, and circumstances change and evolve and, I'm sorry to say, expensive emergencies happen.

> "HOW MUCH MONEY WILL I NEED TO RETIRE?"
>
> EVERYONE'S FIRST QUESTION

Turning the QUESTION
on Its Head

During careers that have seen us advise more than 4,000 clients, Pat McClain and I have developed a process for determining retirement readiness based on each person's unique seven personal decision points. So when someone asks the "How much?" question, the advisement process actually begins in earnest with my turning it on its head by asking each and every caller an equally direct question: "After you retire, how do you intend to pay your bills?"

> ## "HOW DO YOU INTEND TO PAY YOUR BILLS AFTER YOU RETIRE?"
>
> ### SCOTT HANSON

About 99 percent of the time my question takes people by surprise. They've just asked me something, and they were expecting a specific answer, such as "Mrs. Jones, my crystal ball tells me that it's going to take $700,000 for you to retire comfortably in Seattle, Washington, in the year 2017."

While, sadly, there are no crystal balls, there is a process. And because you're reading *Personal Decision Points*, and because we need to begin to refine *your* process, I'm asking you *right now*, how do you intend to pay your bills after you retire?

If your answer is "I plan to live off my savings and Social Security," that's understandable. In fact, it's by far the most common reply I hear.

But that doesn't mean it's the best answer.

It's not the best answer because you *absolutely* do not want to retire and then steadily deplete your savings. In fact, ideally, the majority of your savings should remain intact for the duration of your life. And here's where *7 Personal Decision*

Points comes in: If you plan correctly and follow the steps outlined in these pages, not only is a slowed-down depletion of your savings possible, but entering into retirement with an increased level of confidence should become your expectation.

Two Big Reasons to PRESERVE Your Savings

The reasons you shouldn't deplete your savings principal will be covered throughout *Personal Decision Points*, but here are a couple of biggies: First, you have no idea how long you are going to live. If you use your principal to pay your day-to-day expenses, my experience has been that it's quite possible you'll run out of money.

Second, you have no idea what types of emergencies, be they medical, legal, or familial, you're going to have, and those emergencies can cost you tens of thousands of dollars.

All of this means that in a very real sense, you aren't just preparing for retirement, you're preparing for the unexpected. And after almost 25 years as an advisor, *the one thing I can predict* is that emergencies happen to almost everyone, and these emergencies are almost always shockingly expensive.

Building Mountains of STABILITY

After you've retired and rolled over your 401(k), or, for those fortunate few, received a lump-sum pension from your employer—an amount that is quite likely more money than you've ever had in your life—it's normal to think that your mountain of money is going to last forever.

But it's not that simple. To preserve your savings, serious planning is required.

And we believe (serious) planning begins when you select a qualified, credentialed investment advisor who can give you an accurate evaluation of your circumstances, create a reasonable budget, and provide expert investment advice that takes into account both your short- and long-term goals and personal risk tolerances.

Again, we firmly believe that without this structure in place, you risk becoming one of the 60 percent of *prepared* Americans who runs out of money years before they die.

MONEY VERSUS LONGEVITY
life after retirement

money	●	●	●	●	·	·	·											
health	●	●	●	●	●	●	●	●	●	●	●	●	●	●	·	·	·	·
	63	64	65	66	67	68	69	70	71	72	73	74	75	76	77	78	79	80

CALCULATING Your Retirement Income Needs

Determining how much income you'll need when you retire is a complex process. Some well-intentioned studies state that you'll need to earn between 70 percent and 80 percent of your current income to make it work, but the fact is that

"YOUR GOAL
SHOULD BE TO
USE THE MONEY
YOU'VE SAVED, BE IT
FROM YOUR 401(K),
COMPANY PENSION,
INVESTMENTS,
INHERITANCE OR
OTHER SOURCE,
NOT TO LIVE ON,
BUT TO GENERATE
THE INCOME, OR A
PORTION OF THE
INCOME, THAT YOU
INTEND TO LIVE OFF
FOR THE REST OF
YOUR LIFE."

SCOTT HANSON

some people need more than that to fund extra expenses such as new hobbies, travel, increased healthcare costs, the addition of grandchildren to the family, and so on.

The first thing we need to do is to define the means by which you will earn money once you retire. Here are a handful of ways you'll likely replace the income from your working years:

- Income generated from investments
- Pension
- Social Security
- Rental income
- Inheritance
- Part-time or full-time work

While everyone's financial situation is unique, I find it helpful to utilize examples that touch upon the things that most of us will face. Here's a real-life story that should help you understand the process of calculating your retirement income needs.

A few weeks ago I met with a new client who is 60 years old and hoping to retire at age 66. Joe had amassed about $1 million in his company savings plan.

Joe has worked for the same company for almost 30 years and has been earning about $100,000 per year. His kids are all grown and on their own, he's single, and he has a modest mortgage on his home. Based upon his current savings and a reasonable growth assumption, just off the top of my head I estimated his 401(k) could well be worth as much as $1.6 million in 6 years when he's due to retire.

Joe, Bill, Sue, and the **4 PERCENT** Rule

There have been plenty of academic studies on the 4 Percent Rule. While I'm not typically a huge fan of this rule, for the sake of our example, and because there is no single approach to meeting your retirement income needs, applying the 4 Percent Rule here will work just fine.

Briefly, the 4 Percent Rule states that, based on our current low-interest-rate environment, a 4 percent annual withdrawal from savings is probably safe because there's a reasonable expectation of earning a 4 percent annual return on a properly diversified, moderate-risk portfolio.

Simply put, according to the rule, a 4 percent return on investments, subtracting 4 percent for expenses = no depletion of principal.

So, based on Joe's projected $1.6 million saved, 4 percent would amount to $64,000 in annual income with no depletion of principal.

Good for Joe! He's all set, right?

Not. So. Fast.

While $64,000 a year may sound reasonable, when I presented this number to him, Joe's face dropped like a bag of hammers. That's because he'd grown so used to knowing what he could and what he could not afford to do on his $100,000 income, he didn't want to take a 36 percent pay reduction in order to retire.

This is actually a pretty common concern.

To help put Joe's mind at ease, we needed to figure out how to keep his income at $100,000.

We discussed a number of options, such as using a Social Security Bridge (he'd take a little extra money out of his investments in the short term, with the intention of reducing the withdrawals later when he began taking Social Security). And then we discussed the possibility of supplementing his income with part-time work once he retired, but, as outlined with Bill and Sue, you can't count on the future of your health.

In the end, we decided that the best course of action was to be proactive. We immediately increased his 401(k) deposits, began contributing to a Roth IRA, and then agreed to reevaluate his status on a yearly basis. Because the $100,000 income number was what Joe deemed to be his most important "comfort level" stat, it took priority over everything else in the decision-making process.

> **"BUDGETS ARE USEFUL, BUT THEIR PRIMARY FUNCTION SHOULD BE AS A TOOL FOR MANAGING EXPENSES."**
>
> **SCOTT HANSON**

While $1.6 million may seem like a reasonable amount, there's very little room for error. It's a new era in retirement, with pensions increasingly a thing of the past. People like Joe are entirely responsible for amassing the assets necessary to fund their futures. This

"AS YOU READ
THE 7 PERSONAL
DECISION POINTS,
BE PREPARED
TO ANSWER THE
TOUGH QUESTIONS,
QUESTIONS THAT
ARE GOING TO
HELP MAKE YOUR
RETIREMENT THE
KIND OF RETIREMENT,
AND LIFE, THAT
YOU WANT."

SCOTT HANSON

means your retirement income will likely consist of whatever you are able to save, combined with whatever Social Security provides.

Simply, you *not only* have to build your nest egg, you have to make it last.

BUDGET-Based Income Planning

Well-intentioned people often try to determine their retirement needs by coming up with a spending budget and working backward. They calculate how much they'll need for their mortgage, taxes, insurance, food, entertainment, and so on, and then come up with the amount they'll need to meet those expenses.

But the fact is that few people are willing to live on a strict budget. Don't get me wrong, budgets are useful, but their primary function should be as a tool for managing expenses.

A Better Way to CALCULATE Your Retirement Income Needs

Rather than merely try to figure out what your budget totals are going to be so you can then calculate your retirement income needs, my preferred approach is to take your current income level and then back out nonrecurring expenses.

As an example, let's revisit our friend Joe. His annual income is $100,000, and he hasn't saved anything outside of his 401(k). He has no consumer debt (credit card debt or other unsecured loans), so we can assume that he's not living beyond his current means. That's good! But because he's not saving more than what's going into his company savings plan—his 401(k)—we know that he's not living much below his means, either.

Joe's Retirement Income
NEEDS Calculated

Joe's been taking 10 percent of his pre-tax income and having it deposited into his 401(k). So, at first blush, it appears that he'd need to generate 90 percent of his current income during retirement to avoid depleting his savings.

90%
remaining

$100,000
− 401(k)
$90,000

STEP #1 RESULTS

$100,000	Pre-tax annual income
−$10,000	Contributions to 401(k)
$90,000	90% of annual income to be replaced

But there are other costs that Joe currently incurs that he won't have during retirement. One of the big ones is his FICA (Social Security and Medicare) tax, which total 7.65 percent of his income.

"WHILE HAVING NO CONSUMER DEBT TYPICALLY SHOWS THAT YOU ARE NOT LIVING BEYOND YOUR MEANS, IT DOESN'T INDICATE ANYTHING ABOUT YOUR SAVINGS FOR RETIREMENT."

SCOTT HANSON

If we subtract the 10 percent that goes into his 401(k), and the 7.65 percent that goes toward his FICA taxes, the total amount of income he needs to replace is now 82.35 percent.

STEP #2 RESULTS

$100,000	Pre-tax annual income
–$10,000	Contributions to 401(k)
–$7,650	FICA taxes
$82,350	82.35% of annual income to be replaced

What else can we find?

Well, it turns out that Joe has some other expenses that he won't have during retirement. He's been in the same house for a number of years and, while he appreciates the low interest rate on his mortgage, he'd really like to have it paid off by the time he stops working. (Living without a mortgage is an important retirement goal for many people, and we will cover the pros and cons of paying off the mortgage in the following chapters. Hint: There are scenarios where paying off the mortgage is actually not the best option.) To have his mortgage paid off by the time he reaches age 66, Joe's been paying a little extra on it each month.

Joe's current mortgage payment, excluding property taxes and insurance, is about $1,300. After it's paid off, he'll be ahead each month by $1,300, or $15,600 annually. This equates to 15.6 percent of his income!

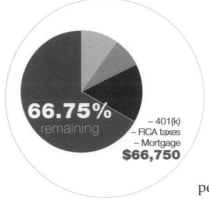

66.75%
remaining
$66,750
– 401(k)
– FICA taxes
– Mortgage

After we back out the 401(k) deposits ($10,000), the FICA taxes ($7,650), and the mortgage payments ($15,600), we find that the percentage of Joe's income that needs to be replaced in retirement is now 66.75 percent ($66,750) of his current salary.

STEP #3 RESULTS

$100,000	Pre-tax annual income
–$10,000	Contributions to 401(k)
–$7,650	FICA taxes
–$15,600	Mortgage
$66,750	66.75% of annual income to be replaced

We've calculated that by the time he retires, Joe should have roughly $1.6 million in his 401(k), and a 4 percent return (which is reasonable) on $1.6 million is $64,000.

These calculations put Joe at just about 100 percent of his pre-retirement income. (For reasons I'll address throughout *Personal Decision Points*, these totals intentionally don't include Joe's Social Security.)

A **CAUTION** about Social Security

While it would seem accounting for Social Security would be a good buffer against the loss of a few percentage points in returns (and subsequent dollars of income), I firmly believe that several steps of changes to the program are on the way.

Some of these changes could drastically impact you.

Why do I believe this? Here's an example from just a short time ago. In November of 2015, with no prior warning, Congress and the president decided to put an end to the popular "File and Suspend" Social Security claiming strategy.

Tens of thousands of people will be adversely affected by this legislation.

Briefly, in marriages or domestic partnerships, File and Suspend allowed the higher income earner (so long as they had achieved full retirement age) to file for Social Security, but then turn around and suspend the payments. This allowed the person to receive higher monthly payments at a future date, while their spouse could immediately start receiving a monthly amount that was half of what the full retirement-age Social Security recipient's payments would have been.

Over the span of the average retirement, this nifty filing strategy enabled some people to earn more than $130,000 in extra income.

What I'm saying is that additional changes and future restrictions to Social Security are likely. And these cuts will almost certainly impact people like Joe, who are deemed to have adequate available resources.

I don't want to be an alarmist, but the fact is that tens of thousands of people were taken by surprise by the sudden demise of File and Suspend. Those people were counting on that income. So, given the scope of the Social Security budget shortfall, along with the government's inability to live within its means, it's not difficult to imagine people with as little as $500,000 saved could actually fail a future Social Security means test and be subjected to reduced (or even eliminated) benefits.

Joe, Bill & Sue, and **YOU**

So what do Joe, Bill, and Sue all have in common? By most eyeball tests, those three would appear to have accumulated enough assets to retire comfortably. But the difference between them is that Bill and Sue came to us after they were *forced* to retire—years before they expected to leave the asset accumulation stage—while Joe was able to plan his transition in advance.

Remember: It's not just about the amount of money you've saved, it's about evaluating your entire financial picture—your assets, tax liabilities, income sources, fixed expenses, and your goals and dreams.

Yes, it's complex. But it's also very simple: If you don't plan, no amount of money can protect you. Conversely, if you work with a credentialed, qualified professional, a person who has your best interests in mind, the odds of you living the retirement of your dreams may increase exponentially.

EXPENSES AND DEBT MANAGEMENT

IN THIS CHAPTER
YOU WILL LEARN...

- *The importance of covering fixed costs with fixed income*

- *The advantage of retiring debt-free*

- *An introduction to managing a mortgage in retirement*

Introduction

I want you to consider a phrase my business partner Pat McClain is fond of saying, "Money that is not going out is the same as money coming in."

Pat regularly comes up with these bits of wisdom, and I have to admit that the very first time I heard him say this, I looked at him sideways (as I often do). In fact, for all of five seconds or so, I wasn't *completely* sure what he meant.

But once it became clear, the simple truth of that statement has never left me.

As you read this chapter, and as you consider your own financial situation—*especially*

> ## "MONEY THAT IS NOT GOING OUT IS THE SAME AS MONEY COMING IN."
> **PAT MCCLAIN**

in regard to any money you may owe, your retirement, and how you are going to pay your debts and expenses—it's my hope that you, too, will understand that, yes, money that is NOT going out is very much the same as money coming in.

Cover **FIXED** Costs with **FIXED** Income

The second key Personal Decision Point in your retirement transition is concerned with the correlation between debt, expenses, and maintaining a healthy post-work financial life.

First, let's gain a better understanding of your "fixed" or "hard" expenses.

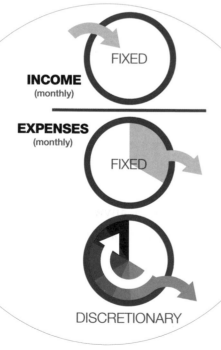

The fact is that far too many people have no idea what their hard expenses are. One of the most important yet least-understood aspects of your retirement transition is the importance of knowing precisely where your money is going. Once you understand where your money is going and how you are going to cover those costs, you can quickly learn how to keep more of it for yourself.

Fixed
COSTS

Let's discuss fixed costs, or the expenses that you *have* to pay on a regular basis, such as utilities, insurance, mortgage, property taxes, and so on.

Fixed costs, of course, are money that is headed out your wide-open front door.

Fixed income is income you get from a pension or investment that is set at a particular figure, which doesn't vary or rise with the rate of inflation.

Basically, it's consistent, *guaranteed* income.

I always advise people to arrange their lives to cover fixed expenses with fixed income.

There are several reasons for this, but chief among them is that you can always skip a vacation, or a dinner out on the town, which means your discretionary spending can vary greatly from week to week and month to month. But you can't just decide to *not* pay your electric bill for too long before someone knocks on your door and shuts off your power.

My experience has been that, pretty much anywhere you live, an extra vacation is easier to bypass than a winter without heat.

But let's assume it won't ever get to that.

What I'm encouraging you to do is to make your life easier. When you put yourself in the position to cover your "have to" expenses with guaranteed income, you're *not only* conserving your savings principal, but you're weather-proofing yourself against unexpected storms.

Here's a list of common fixed expenses:

- Mortgage (or rent, timeshares, or leases)
- Insurance
- Utilities
- Service payments (cable television)
- Real estate taxes
- Alimony

As introduced in Chapter 1, it's paramount to begin your retirement while you're in a position to preserve your principal. This means knowing your expenses, limiting your debt, and covering your costs, whatever they are, with income derived through diversified portfolio investment management, along with fixed income.

Fixed **INCOME** Strategies

Let's take a closer look. A portfolio that includes fixed income is generally one that has low-risk funds such as bonds or bond mutual funds that pay regular dividends or interest that you can count on. You might have several sources of income to consider when approaching retirement: IRAs, 401(k)s, Social Security, pensions, investment accounts, money market funds, and CDs.

A well-balanced financial portfolio going into retire-ment for many people includes investments that will yield some degree of stable income stream. You can work with your financial advisor to make the best choices for your personal retirement—and I certainly advise you to do this as the financial environment is both ever-changing and con-fusing even to the most savvy money-minded folks.

> **"COVER FIXED EXPENSES WITH FIXED INCOME."**
>
> **SCOTT HANSON**

Fixed income strategies can include these options:

- Optimizing returns according to interest rates
- Diversifying by blending bonds with consecu-tive maturities
- Investing in short-, medium-, or long-duration investments
- Investing in equities
- Participating in real estate investment traded trusts (REITs)
- Investing in inflation-protected securities

Keep in mind: Interest rates change, and as they rise, bond prices generally fall; as interest rates fall, bond prices generally rise. For instance, if it appears we are due to face an interest rate hike, it makes better financial sense to invest in shorter-maturity bond mutual funds.

Work with your financial advisor to determine the right choices for your portfolio—it can make a huge difference for your optimum level of cash flows and maximizing your tax savings.

Debt Management
and LIFESTYLE

DEBT: Something that is owed or due. The state of owing money.

While debt is something that is owed or due, it can, of course, also be a fixed expense. Debt includes loans, such as home mortgages, or car, boat, or student or personal loans, and also includes various types of credit cards and lines of credit. This means that, regardless of what may be happening in your current life—illness, divorce, the death of a loved one, the loss of your job, unexpected major home repairs, accidents—the institution that loaned you the money will insist on being paid.

The scary truth about the state of debt in our country is that we Americans are once again getting better at digging ourselves a deeper debt hole. According to a December 2015 report by the Board of Governors of the Federal Reserve System, over the past three years American consumer credit debt increased at an annual rate of 5½ percent. Revolving credit—that is, the kind of credit in which the monthly balance and minimum payments can fluctuate—has increased at an annual rate of ¼ percent, while non-revolving credit (such as car loans) has increased at an annual rate of 7½ percent!

> ## "DO NOT SAVE WHAT IS LEFT AFTER SPENDING, SPEND WHAT IS LEFT AFTER SAVING."
> **WARREN BUFFETT**

While this can be good for the economy in the short term, boiled down to the average debt per U.S. household, it comes to a whopping $16,140 in credit cards, $155,361 in home mortgages, and $31,946 in student loans.

Let's face it: We need to stop this runaway debt train because these burdens must eventually be paid.

Pay It OFF

Priority #1 should be to look at all your outstanding credit card debt and determine how you can consolidate your payments and whittle those down so that you are no longer getting gouged with interest fees—or worse, just mak-

PRIORITY #1

ing payments that cover accrued interest. Rather than contribute to a bad statistic, strive to get to the point where you only use your credit cards when you can pay them off every month. Then make it a rule to use them strictly for convenience, or benefits such as frequent flier miles or affinity program advantages.

Don't take it personally, but when it comes to your creditors, you're a number on a spreadsheet, and whether or not you can afford to make the payment is completely irrelevant to the finance company.

This is why I am a huge advocate of helping people retire debt-free. Debt not only limits your freedom, it moves you closer to the fiscal cliff in the event something bad happens and you can't pay your fixed expenses.

So, as you prepare for retirement, take a look at all the loans you have. How much is owed on the mortgage? Do you have auto loans (or leases)? How many and for how much? Are there balances on your credit cards? How much? (I want you to be thinking about those debts, and I suggest that you get out a piece of paper and list them now.)

Once you have compiled a list of all of your debts, write down the total of all your obligations, and then calculate the total of all your monthly payments.

There are three things to look for here:

- First, total debt: How much is going out each month?

- Second, cash flow: If you paid off your debt, how many more hundreds or thousands of dollars in disposable income would you have each month?

- Third: If you paid your debt down faster (for example, by increasing your payments by just 15 percent), how much in interest would you save over the next three years?

Even though I will advise you time and again to do everything you can to pay off your debt, I also firmly believe that getting in the habit of setting aside savings while you simultaneously pay down debt is not only possible but can make a huge difference in relieving debt anxiety and providing you with some added security.

> "A MAN IN DEBT IS SO FAR A SLAVE."
>
> RALPH WALDO EMERSON

The **ADVANTAGE** of
Retiring Debt-Free

I've found that most people who have debt really don't understand it. They have $1 million in home equity, retirement accounts, and other real estate, and they have $250,000 in debt (don't forget the interest each month). These people think they are fine! Yet when you retire and have, for instance, $600,000 from a pension rollover or 401(k), and you have income (from investments and Social Security), and you have zero debt, you are in a much better position than someone who retires with $1 million yet has a huge mortgage and other debt siphoning off $7,000 (or more) each month.

But the reality is that not everyone can manage to pay off his or her debt before hitting retirement. I understand this, and we have to be reasonable based on each individual's unique situation. So here's another important key to a successful retirement: If you simply can't pay off your debt before you retire, then once you enter retirement, restructure your debts to make your payments as low as possible.

Restructuring your debts to be as low as possible is a strategic approach that will make a huge difference in your retirement life.

Remember what Pat McClain said: Money NOT going out is the same as money coming in.

How to **RESTRUCTURE** Your Debt Before and After Retirement

Let's take a look at debt and retirement a little more closely. Let's assume that you have a mortgage on your home with a balance of $200,000, and it's seven years un-

"MANY PEOPLE TAKE NO CARE OF THEIR MONEY TILL THEY COME NEARLY TO THE END OF IT, AND OTHERS DO JUST THE SAME WITH THEIR TIME."

JOHANN WOLFGANG VON GOETHE

til you retire. If the loan is still in existence after you stop working, you'll be stuck with the same monthly mortgage payment you currently have. However, if you apply extra principal payments now with each and every monthly bill, your loan balance will be less when you transition into retirement. (And, providing your mortgage allows for this, you could re-amortize this debt in exchange for a much lower payment.)

So, big idea #1: While you are working, pay as much as possible to get your debts paid down. Zero debt is the goal. But the second-best option is to eliminate as many debts as possible and to lower your overall payments and interest amounts.

Your debt and retirement goals:

- Zero debt upon retirement.

- If you can't make it to zero by the time you retire, restructure your debts, including refinancing your home to lower the interest rate and/or extend the loan to 15 or even 30 years.

This is because cash flow during retirement is king.

To repeat: Most people benefit when they retire without a mortgage. So, I usually advise clients to "up" their monthly mortgage payments to get their house paid off by the time they retire. However, for those whose mortgages are too large to pay off by the time they stop working, after they retire, I advise them to restructure their loans—even if that loan has as little as five or seven years remaining on it—and re-amortize it out to 15, 20, or even 30 years.

When Paying Off the Mortgage Is **NOT** the Best Course of Action

Here's a brief example of a recent caller to our financial topic radio program, *Money Matters*. Bob and Joanne are married, retired, both 69, and have a combined monthly income of $6,000 from Social Security, an annuity, and a small pension. Their monthly fixed expenses are as follows:

BOB AND JOANNE'S MONTHLY FIXED EXPENSES:

$1,800	Mortgage (7 years remaining)
$1,200	Various insurance coverages
$500	Utilities
$800	Credit card payments
$400	Taxes
$4,700	Total fixed expenses

They both desperately wanted to travel and enjoy life more, but in their current situation, with fixed expenses of $4,700 covered by their fixed income (and practically no other savings), that left them with just $1,300 a month for food, travel, and discretionary expenditures. (Which explained the high credit card debt.)

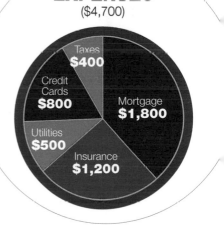

FIXED EXPENSES
($4,700)

Taxes **$400**

Credit Cards **$800**

Mortgage **$1,800**

Utilities **$500**

Insurance **$1,200**

In situations such as this, many people simply opt to get a second mortgage. (A reverse mortgage or downsizing were both possibilities here, but for various reasons I advised them to go a different direction.) While a second mortgage would leave them with cash and pay their expenses for a while, it would raise their mortgage to $3,000 or more. So this is what I recommended: Because they were determined to stay in their home (they have almost $350,000 in equity), I had them refinance their mortgage for 30 years, which lowered their monthly payment to $600 a month. I recommended they take that $1,200 savings, apply it to their credit cards, along with any extra money they could find, so they could pay off that debt within one year.

With nothing more than that, within one year they would have an additional $2,000 in fixed income (and $2,000 less in fixed expenses) each month.

Then they could start living the life they wanted and also feel a bit more secure.

Now, there are some exceptions to this strategy. Let's say you have an income stream that will end in a specific number of years. Maybe you've sold a piece of property for which you carried the loan for the buyer, or you have an annuity that will cease at a particular date in the future. If a scenario such as this applies to you, then a good strategy is to structure a debt payoff that coincides with the ending of the income stream.

DOUBLE-CHECK Your Debt Management Plan

Debt is the largest killer of retirement dreams.

1. Pay off the house BEFORE retirement. If you are ten years from retirement, even if your loan is longer, amortize to pay off your house before you stop working.

2. If you are going to need to make changes to your dwelling, such as downsizing or major repairs or upgrades, do them before you retire.

We often survey callers, clients, and people who attend our workshops, asking them questions related to debt and lifestyle. We asked a recently retired husband and wife team, what's the most difficult thing for you? They said: The day we realized that we were no longer saving for retirement and were no longer receiving a paycheck, and that all of a sudden the money we had saved we were now relying upon forever.

Conclusion

Just financially speaking, retirement is a tough transition. No doubt about it, the life changes that come with it can be seriously daunting, and mistakes can cost you dearly at a time when it's tougher to recover.

While you can't control emergencies, you can absolutely control your expenses and your debt. I've said it before and I'll say it again:

- Cover your fixed expenses with fixed income.

- Retire debt-free, but if you can't (there are exceptions) then lower your monthly payments, even if you have to extend the loans by several years.

- Money that is NOT going out is the same as money coming in.

Even if you have a button-down debt management plan, it can pay—emotionally and financially—to work with a qualified, credentialed advisor that you can trust. These are complex times for retirees, and a little hand-holding with an expert who is looking out for you can go a long way.

TAX PLANNING

IN THIS CHAPTER YOU WILL LEARN...

- *How tax planning can save you thousands*

- *An introduction to Social Security tax concerns*

- *Tips for retirement tax planning*

The **AIRTIGHT CASE** for Careful Retirement Tax Planning

Right up front I want to make it very clear that I am not an accountant. No one except an expert in tax law should give you advice about tax planning. What I'm offering here is an overview based on my experience, as well as some suggestions and scenarios that will hopefully instill in you the sense that your retirement transition is a complex process that requires a "team approach." And it is my opinion that your team should include an experienced, qualified, credentialed accountant.

That said, there's not a week that goes by that an advisor at Hanson McClain doesn't meet with a retiree who has been paying significantly more in taxes than they needed to. I'm not talking about overpayments of a few hundred dollars. These overpayments are very different from when a self-employed person pays too much in quarterly estimates, or when someone has too much withheld from their paycheck.

In those cases, the IRS will issue a refund.

The problem is that while the tax laws pertaining to retirees are frustratingly complex, I still regularly encounter pre-retirees and retirees who have undertaken no long-term tax planning whatsoever. And this lack of planning results in unnecessary (and shockingly high) tax bills.

> ## "YOUR TAX PLANNING DESERVES AS MUCH CARE AS YOUR INVESTING."
>
> ### SCOTT HANSON

Let me be clear, by "shockingly high" I mean they've paid tens of thousands of dollars more than they should have.

The fact is that I've received calls from dozens of people just in the last few years whose total net worth was less than $700,000, and yet who had unwittingly paid as much as $30,000 to the IRS that could have been saved with preemptive tax planning.

And the worst part is that once *this* type of money goes to the IRS, there's usually no getting it back.

Making sometimes-massive overpayments is a trap even the most savvy retirees can fall into. Navigating the maze of retirement tax planning requires mastering the complexities of tax laws, along with how the timing of each decision will affect a particular retiree's standard of living.

But with a tax code over 70,000 pages long, it's never simple.

Tax preparation when you are working is one thing, as your tax liability is generally based on your income.

But tax planning during retirement is completely different. Retirees have migrated from the wide-open plains to the Amazon rainforest, with rules and regulations that they never had to be concerned with at age 30. Take one path, and your tax liability plummets. Take a different path, and you're faced with a monster tax bill.

What Is **PREEMPTIVE** Tax Planning?

Preemptive tax planning is not some shifty shell game that employs gray-area methodologies or a suspension of your ethics.

Not at all.

Proper retirement transition tax planning takes into account all the different parts of your financial life. This important area of planning considers the *when, where,* and *how* of your income, investments, and purchases, along with your filings and deductions.

Here are some of the specific items to consider in preemptive tax planning:

- **When** distributions are taken
- **When** major purchases are made

- **What** amounts are distributed
- **What** type of accounts are used
- **Which** types of investments are chosen
- **Which** account distributions are taken (taxable or non-taxable)
- **Why** some deductions are superior to others
- **Where** you live (which state)

HOW It Saves You Money

In an approach that has always struck me as upside down, people will spend hundreds or thousands of hours over the course of their lives choosing and monitoring their investment portfolios. (Of course, I'm *completely* on board with the careful allocation of your hard-earned money.)

Yet after they retire, other than saving receipts and scheduling an appointment with their accountant, when it comes to monitoring their income taxes they do almost no planning.

This. Drives. Me. Crazy.

Here's why: A great investment strategy *should* result in a few increased percentage points and improved investment returns. But a great tax strategy can actually be 10 percent or even 20 percent more advantageous.

Preemptive Planning Helps Make **EARNERS** into **KEEPERS**

Many retirees have multiple sources of income. The universal source is Social Security, which may be taxable. (It's the sources and amounts of the *other* income you receive during retirement that determine whether you have to pay taxes on your Social Security.)

Two other common income sources are IRAs and employer-sponsored savings accounts such as a 401(k). Income from these sources is taxed when the money is withdrawn. (Some retirees, of course, derive income from rentals or small businesses, while still others receive interest from savings, investments, and capital gains.)

These are the standard retirement income sources:

- Social Security
- IRAs
- Employer-sponsored retirement accounts
- Savings
- Investments
- Inheritances
- Capital gains
- Real estate
- Small businesses

Common wisdom suggests that during your working years you defer as much of your income as possible into an employer-sponsored savings plan, such as a 401(k) or 403(b). This strategy works great for reducing taxes while a person is employed because the money isn't considered taxable income. By deferring income, people can amass large sums for retirement. But, of course, all of these accumulated dollars will eventually be taxed. And then, unfortunately, because of a lack of planning, many retirees will end up paying higher taxes *during retirement* than while they were working—thus negating all or some of the advantages of having deferred the taxes!

For example, if you saved pre-tax money when your federal or state tax rate was at one level, but taxes go on to increase to a higher rate once you retire (or laws regarding distributions change), you'll wind up paying more. Alternatively, the amount of your distributions—your reward for years of saving—may nudge you into a higher tax bracket than when you were working.

It's a confusing mess, to say the least.

Another factor that makes the planning process so tricky is the progressive tax system we have in the United States.

Under our current system, a middle-class retiree who withdraws money from her retirement account could be taxed on that distribution at a rate ranging from what a person in poverty would pay (zero), to what the CEO of a Fortune 500 company would pay.

"THE ONLY DIFFERENCE BETWEEN DEATH AND TAXES IS THAT DEATH DOESN'T GET WORSE EVERY TIME CONGRESS MEETS."

WILL ROGERS

Far too often (based on things like how much is withdrawn, or even *when* it's taken) I see people getting taxed as though they're fat cats when in reality their retirement income is extremely modest. That inequality exists because the tax rate is based on a mind-numbing combination of laws and individual scenarios.

What follows are a few short examples of how you can utilize tax planning to help save your hard-earned money.

EXAMPLE #1:
AN UNEXPECTED BITE BY THE TAX SHARK

Recently I met a couple that had retired and wanted to pay off their mortgage. They liked the idea of having fewer obligations during retirement, and they very much wanted to be debt-free. (As shown throughout *Personal Decision Points*, being debt-free is an important *pre-retirement* goal.) This couple's mortgage balance was about $200,000, a seemingly manageable amount compared to the almost $1,000,000 they had saved in their IRAs and 401(k).

When the husband retired from his job, he contacted his employer's HR department to learn about withdrawal options from his 401(k). He was told that because he had retired, he could have access to his funds (he was over age 55), and there would be no early withdrawal penalties. He asked about the tax ramifications, and the well-meaning customer service representative on the other end of the phone told him that there would be a 20 percent federal income tax withholding.

After doing what he felt was his due diligence, the husband requested a $250,000 withdrawal from his 401(k) so he could pay off their mortgage. The plan administrator withheld the 20 percent for taxes and then sent the remaining $200,000 to him. Upon receipt of the money, the couple paid off their home and celebrated by enjoying a fancy dinner with an expensive bottle of wine.

This should be a heart-warming story of a deserving couple who worked hard their entire lives, saved their money, and entered retirement debt-free and with a nice nest egg of $750,000 in savings.

Unfortunately, the story doesn't end there.

A few months later their accountant informed them that they owed an *additional* $58,000 in taxes, despite already having paid $50,000! They were hit with a huge tax bill because the IRS considered the $250,000 withdrawal regular income for that tax year.

Not only did the withdrawal push their income from the 15 percent tax bracket to the 27 percent tax bracket, it also eliminated their ability to deduct their personal exemptions *while simultaneously* reducing the amount of their itemized deductions. (It may sound confusing, but this

PAYING OFF DEBT
(costly mistake-all in 1 year)

1 YEAR

401(k)

TAX

INC. TAX

IRA

type of scenario is surprisingly common.) All that, and the withdrawal also triggered much higher *state* income taxes.

Unfortunately, by the time this couple came to see me, there was little I could do. You simply can't undo the tax bill for the previous year by returning the money to the 401(k).

The only thing left that we could do was to plan wisely on how they would come up with the $58,000 that was being demanded by the IRS.

How They Could've **AVOIDED** the Tax Bite

Paying off the mortgage could have been accomplished in a variety of ways, and would have saved them thousands of dollars. The best solution would depend upon everything else that was going on in their financial lives.

Briefly, if they'd had cash savings that weren't locked up in an IRA, 401(k), or other retirement plan, those after-tax dollars could have been used without triggering such a large tax bill.

But with all of their retirement savings in retirement plan accounts, a better approach to paying off their home would have been this: They could have transferred the 401(k) to an IRA *before* taking a series of withdrawals (over a few years) in order to minimize their tax liability.

While this approach may seem a bit complicated, it would be nothing new for a competent advisor, and it's certainly an effective way to preserve money. In fact, this little alteration would also have saved them thousands of dollars.

The four-year strategy would have been accomplished by establishing a separate IRA with the sole purpose of paying off the home. For example, $250,000 could have been transferred from the 401(k) to the IRA. No taxes would be due at this stage because this would be a direct transfer rather than a withdrawal. Then, for the current year, and the subsequent three years, a monthly withdrawal would be set up that would be used to make *accelerated* mortgage payments. The extra payments would go to pay down the mortgage principal so that the house would be mortgage-free in four years.

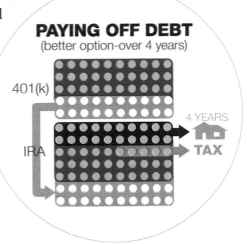

PAYING OFF DEBT
(better option-over 4 years)

401(k)

IRA

4 YEARS

TAX

EXAMPLE #2:
CAGING THE TAX SHARK

On a happier note, another couple I recently worked with was able to avoid a similar costly experience. A number of years ago, before becoming my clients, these folks moved from California to Texas to escape my home state's infamously high income taxes. (The top tax rate in California stands at 13.3 percent, while Texas has zero state income tax.)

The couple spent the majority of their time in Texas, and maintained a smaller residence in California for visiting family. This lifestyle worked out great until one of their elderly parents needed round-the-clock care back in California.

It was time to move back home.

When they came to me, they were just days away from selling their Texas house. Once the escrow closed on that house, they would no longer be residents of zero-state-income-tax Texas.

This couple was receiving monthly disbursements from their IRAs, which constituted a majority of their retirement income. If they continued to receive money each month after moving back to California, their IRA withdrawals would be subject to the high tax rates of California.

After reviewing their situation, I advised them to take a large withdrawal mid-year from their IRA and to cease monthly withdrawals as soon as they were no longer residents of Texas. While they won't be able to avoid California income taxes like this forever, this simple step saved them $15,000.

As shown in these two examples, creative tax planning can help you preserve the money you've saved for retirement. The main problem, as illustrated in example #1, is that when you wait too long to consult an expert, you reduce your options.

Once you commit yourself to any financial endeavor, whether selling your house or withdrawing funds after retirement, you're locked into the complex laws and restrictions that are created to derive revenue for the government.

When it comes to taxes, what's good for the government may not be so good for you.

Make sure you consult a professional before you make any big moves. It could save you thousands of dollars and a lot of frustration down the road.

Social Security
TAX BASICS

Social Security, America's financial safety net, appears to be a straightforward plan based on your lifetime earnings. Because a slight majority of retirees *currently* pay no income tax on their Social Security benefits, you might think that advance tax planning is unnecessary.

But the criteria are subject to change.

Case in point: According to the Social Security Administration, by 2030, it's estimated that 58 percent of all Social Security recipients will be paying taxes on their benefits.

Think 14 years is too far in the future to be concerned? If you have any income *outside* of Social Security—say, you work a part-time

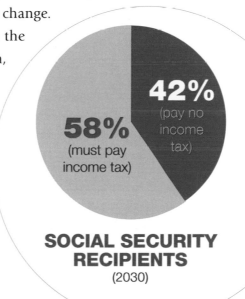

42%
(pay no income tax)

58%
(must pay income tax)

**SOCIAL SECURITY
RECIPIENTS**
(2030)

job, as many people do—then your benefits and tax burden could be affected.

What follows is a fairly common Social Security tax mishap that serves as an introduction to a few things you should watch out for.

EXAMPLE #3:
THE COMPLEX RULES OF SOCIAL SECURITY

One of my clients wanted to convert a portion of his IRA to a Roth IRA. Like many retirees, he was in the 15 percent federal income tax bracket and wanted to avoid getting bumped up into the 25 percent bracket. To achieve this, he carefully calculated how much of his IRA he could convert while still remaining in the lower bracket.

The online calculator he used worked great—except that it failed to take into account his Social Security benefits. His retirement income consisted of a modest pension, some stock dividends, and Social Security. Because his income was below a certain level, he and his wife's Social Security benefits had been tax-free. Although he correctly calculated how much he could convert while remaining in the 15 percent tax bracket, he didn't realize that this conversion resulted in an effective tax rate of 22.5 percent.

Simply, the minute he made the conversion from an IRA to a Roth IRA, that money became taxable as income. That's because the Roth IRA funds combined with his Social Security to raise his income to a level that made half of his Social Security benefits taxable.

Security Through
DIVERSITY

Things can become even trickier when there are other assets apart from IRAs and 401(k)s, such as large positions in stocks or mutual funds, rental real estate, and large cash balances. Although having a variety of assets is more complex, when you're preparing for retirement, that variety allows you to create a diversified savings and tax strategy, just as you should have a diversified investment strategy.

Ideally, you'll reach retirement with a variety of different investment vehicles. A well-rounded retirement portfolio may include a monthly pension, Social Security, dividends from stocks and funds, interest from taxable and tax-free bonds, withdrawals from a post-taxed savings account, and rental income.

Generally, the broader the investment vehicles, the more flexibility you have in regard to tax planning, and, subsequently, the more money you can keep.

> **"THE HARDEST THING TO UNDERSTAND IN THE WORLD IS THE INCOME TAX."**
>
> **ALBERT EINSTEIN**

But you need to plan, because while multiple savings and investment choices can create options, even innocent mistakes can cost you.

Some Essential
REMINDERS for
Retirement Tax Planning

The potential scenarios for proper tax planning are too varied to be concisely listed here. Needless to say, if you have savings and investments, it should be ongoing.

With that in mind, here are some practical concerns:

1. THE AMOUNT AND BLEND OF YOUR INCOME SOURCES IMPACT YOUR TAX LIABILITY.

Are you eligible for, or do you already receive, Social Security? Are you married? Do you file separate or joint returns? Depending on your other income, 50 percent to 85 percent of your Social Security benefits are taxable.

2. DIFFERENT TYPES OF INVESTMENTS ARE TAXED AT DIFFERENT RATES.

The investment opportunities available to you will vary according to your career path. The retirement plans available to State of California employees, for example, are very different from the plans offered by a Fortune 500 company.

Because the following assets are all taxed at unique rates, they'll need to be sheltered differently in your retirement accounts:

- Cash and bonds
- Stock mutual funds

- Individual stocks with large turnover

- ETF and index funds

- Collectibles and precious metals (gold, silver, and platinum are currently taxed at 28 percent!)

Do you or your accountant know the different tax rates? Your risk tolerance and how long you plan to hold an investment should be the basis for determining how to allocate your portfolio.

3. THE TIMING AND AMOUNT OF DISTRIBU-TIONS FROM YOUR VARIOUS ACCOUNTS CAN AFFECT YOUR TAX LIABILITY.

One of the most common mistakes retirees make is to systematically deplete one retirement account in full, draining it month by month, before moving on to the next account. Proper tax planning helps you determine where, when, and how much to withdraw, helping you to maximize your savings while limiting your tax exposure.

4. PRE-TAX PLANS, SUCH AS 401(K)S, CAN BE CHANGED TO POST-TAX ROTH IRAS.

Our tax code allows you to transfer your retirement savings from one type of account (a 401(k), perhaps) to another (a Roth). Even though the transfer of funds from a taxable account to a non-taxable account will require you to pay taxes at the time of the transfer, you will be protecting yourself against future tax liabilities.

5. COMPANY STOCK IN YOUR 401(K) COULD RECEIVE SPECIAL TREATMENT.

Do you own company stock in your 401(k) plan? Has it increased in value? Utilizing net unrealized appreciation may provide you with some worthwhile tax savings. (Be sure to consult a qualified, credentialed investment advisor before undertaking distributions from your employer-sponsored plan.)

The **BOTTOM** Line

These are just a few of the almost limitless possibilities surrounding pre-retiree and retiree tax planning. I could go on about their importance, but rather than drive the point home in any other way, I think the argument has been made, and the clearest endorsement is as follows: Meet with a qualified, credentialed advisor AND a qualified credentialed tax accountant before you begin the retirement transition process. That's because in my more than 25 years as an advisor, I have never once met with a client who didn't financially benefit from pre-emptive tax planning.

INVESTMENT MANAGEMENT

IN THIS CHAPTER YOU WILL LEARN...

- *Why I believe in the long-view approach to investing*

- *How investment diversification can protect you*

- *The importance of understanding your investment risk tolerance profile*

Introduction

After more than 25 years as an advisor, and with the oversight of more than $2 billion in assets, I learned long ago that the single area most likely to derail your transition into retirement is poor investment management.

Organizing your approach is key.

While there have been countless numbers of books written on investing—how to invest, how much to invest, *where* to invest—this book isn't designed to cover the specifics of that process. Conscientious investing should be a part of everyone's retirement preparation, but the individual processes are so personal—encompassing surveys, an appraisal of assets, software applications, research and market analysis, and at least one, if not several meetings, designed to clarify each person's long- and short-term goals—that to try and cover them here would be a waste of time.

So, rather than discuss the specific details of various approaches, I'll instead begin by helping you to attain a firmer grasp of the two most important foundational questions of the investment process:

- What is your risk tolerance? (And what is your level of need to assume risk?)
- What is your time horizon?

Let's look at definitions for both.

RISK TOLERANCE is the degree of variability in investment returns that an individual is willing to withstand.

Let me emphasize that it is vitally important to gain a realistic understanding of your willingness to stomach fluctuations in the value of your investments.

I'll explain why in a moment.

TIME HORIZON is the length of time over which an investment is held before it is liquidated or drawn down by the investor.

Knowing your risk tolerance (what you are willing to lose), while taking into account your time horizon (at what point you'll need your money), should guide each and every decision as you invest for retirement.

Obviously, we would all like to have the highest return with the lowest degree of risk (and in the shortest amount of time). But to be frank, that combination simply doesn't exist as there are no shortcuts and no magic wands.

Deciding just how many ups and downs you can stomach is vitally important. Otherwise, emotional investing takes over, and you are likely to sabotage yourself by selling low when the market drops, and then jumping back in and buying high when the market has risen.

This is one of the most common (and the most damaging) mistakes I see as an advisor.

The urge to invest emotionally happens to the best of us, but becoming intimate with your risk tolerance and time horizon will help you to neutralize the damaging effects of what psychologists and economists call "behavioral finance."

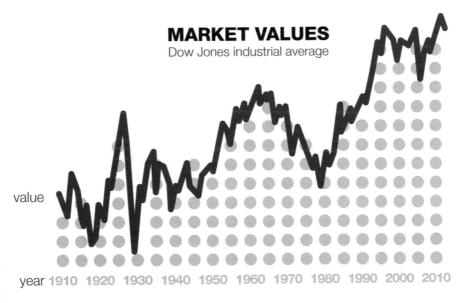

MARKET VALUES
Dow Jones industrial average

value

year 1910 1920 1930 1940 1950 1960 1970 1980 1990 2000 2010

"HOW YOU RESPONDED TO ALL THE VOLATILITY DURING 2000–2009 IS A GREAT WAY TO ASSESS YOUR TRUE RISK TOLERANCE."

SCOTT HANSON

BEHAVIORAL
Finance

When it comes to investing, there are two things that most people fear: First, we don't want to miss out on the next big wave (especially if our friends or neighbors *appear* to be catching that wave). Second, we don't want to be the last one off the sinking ship. Psychologists will argue about which is the greater fear, missing out or staying around for too long. For our purposes, let's just say they are equally terrifying for investors, and let's agree that we are instinctual creatures and prone to invest emotionally.

How these emotions negatively impact your investment decisions is behavioral finance.

If there is one thing that the first decade of this century should have taught us all, it's how we as individual investors respond when markets go berserk. That decade gave us the tech bubble, which caused the broad stock market to plummet almost 50 percent; the real estate bubble, where home prices shot up ridiculously high over a short period of time (only to come crashing down after people loaded up on debt); and the larger financial crisis, which caused just about everything to fall in value.

There were times, such as during 2008, when the market was experiencing all-time record gains and losses—sometimes in the same week—when you could feel the fear in the air.

If you were saving for retirement or investing in the market, not only in 2008 or 2009, but just about any time during the 2000–2009 period, think back to how you felt and reacted to all that turmoil. Accurately and honestly recalling how you responded to all that volatility is one of the best ways to assess your true risk tolerance.

RISK and Investing

First, generally speaking, in order to achieve any rate of return—above the low rates of guaranteed CDs and U.S. Treasuries—you'll need to accept some level of risk.

That is because EVERY investment poses some risk.

Now, in relation to risk, as a side note, it's often said that there is a correlation between rates of return and levels of risk. But that isn't necessarily the case. You can just as easily take on higher risk and still have low returns.

Then, once you come to grips with how much uncertainty, how many ups and downs, you can stomach, it's time to calculate your time horizon. That is, how many years will it be until you'll begin to spend your money (or at least have access to the interest).

However, your actual time horizon may not be precisely when you think.

"RISK IS LIKE FIRE: IF CONTROLLED IT WILL HELP YOU; IF UNCONTROLLED IT WILL RISE UP AND DESTROY YOU."

THEODORE ROOSEVELT

Investing and
ACTUAL Time Horizons

As you approach retirement, you may be tempted to think your time horizon is short. For example, if you plan on retiring in three years, you might think that you'll have a need for your money in three years. But that's often not the case. You may need a *portion* of your money, or you may need to derive some income from your money in three years, but hopefully you won't need all of your principal on the day you retire.

What you *really* need is for your principal to last you the rest of your life. And for that to happen you need your unspent principal to continue to generate income.

After all, while I certainly hope it's for a very long time, you can't know *precisely* how long you're going to live.

But it could very well be quite a while.

Statistics say that, once you hit retirement, you'll probably live a long time. In fact, if you're fortunate enough to

LIFE EXPECTANCY
in 2015

THOSE AGE 65 (in 2015)

male ● · ·
female ● · ·
AGE 65 66 67 68 69 70 71 72 73 74 75 76 77 78 79 80 81 82 83 84 85 86 87

NEWBORN (in 2015)

male ● ● ● ● ● ● ● ● ● ● ● ● ● ● ● · ·
female ● ● ● ● ● ● ● ● ● ● ● ● ● ● ● ● ·
AGE 65 66 67 68 69 70 71 72 73 74 75 76 77 78 79 80 81 82 83

survive until retirement age, your life expectancy is actually longer than people who are born today. (According to the Social Security Administration, the life expectancy for a male who is age 65 today, is 84.3. For a woman, it's 86.6 years! By comparison, the average lifespan of an American born in 2015 is still a shade under 80 years.)

So, although you may be retiring in, say, three years, you'll need your money to last you throughout your retirement, which could be 20 years or more. Naturally, you'll want your money to continue to grow during this period.

This means that most retirees actually have a time horizon that is investment-variable, meaning that your time horizon on this investment might be five years, but on that investment, it's actually ten.

Once you achieve clarity regarding your risk tolerance and your time horizon, there are two overarching principles that you need to adhere to when it comes to investing.

1. YOU AREN'T SMARTER THAN THE MARKET

Wouldn't it be nice to know when the value of a certain investment was about to skyrocket (or fall) in price? It would be great to know when to buy gold and when to sell. Or real estate. Or stocks. Or whatever asset class.

Some people believe that the key to success in retirement investing is to be able to determine where markets are heading. They follow the latest economic reports, watch financial TV every day, read financial analysis, tea leaves, crystal balls, and so on. They think that if they pay close enough attention, they'll figure out the signals and make good buy-and-sell decisions.

The fact is that 99 percent of laymen are unable to accurately determine market movements or even trends. Of course they might get it right some of the time (and of course they'll be sure to let you know all about it). But even if they get it right *some* of the time, one big mistake and they are out of the market completely.

Now consider this: Even if you spend a lot of your time trying to figure out market movements, who are you *really* competing with? Wall Street firms have teams of experts trying to determine market movements. So while you're working on monitoring several different markets, you're competing against not only highly trained and seasoned professionals but their million-dollar software programs as well.

The funny thing is, a majority of the time these experts aren't right, either. In fact, here's a story: I was at a high-level investment conference early in my career. I attended a breakfast session one morning that was hosted by a well-known and highly respected economist. He very confidently presented a case as to why the European stock market was the best place to invest at the time. He had statistics, charts, and graphs, and generally made a compelling argument.

Later that afternoon, I went to another session on the European stock market, but this session was presented by a different expert. This person presented some of the same statistics used by Economist #1 during the breakfast session, but he came up with an entirely different conclusion: He felt that Europe was a terrible place to invest.

So who was I to believe? (Over the next year BOTH turned out to be wrong as the European markets remained pancake flat.)

It was around then that I came away with the conclusion that it would be best to follow long-term financial principles. In short, rather than trying to outsmart the markets, or "time" the markets, it's my opinion that it's much better to simply have "time" in the market.

Simply, you can't outsmart the markets. Don't invest emotionally. Jumping in and jumping out of the market is almost always a mistake. Stay the course, be consistent, and take a long-view approach to investing.

> ## "RATHER THAN 'TIME' THE MARKET, IT'S MUCH BETTER SIMPLY TO HAVE 'TIME' *IN* THE MARKET."
>
> ### SCOTT HANSON

2. DIVERSIFICATION

The second key investment principle is diversification. We've all heard of the importance of remaining diversified, but there's not a week that goes by that I don't encounter someone nearing (or in) retirement who isn't diversified at all. They have all their money in this or that stock or investment.

While a non-diversified retiree investment strategy is worrisome, it's not nearly as common as the #1 area that I encounter where people lack adequate portfolio diversification: their employer's 401(k).

If you work for a publicly traded company, odds are you own stock in that company inside your 401(k). Hey, I understand. You work for that firm. You know about the inner dealings and their core values and philosophy. So you feel that holding stock in the company you work for is a great investment. And perhaps it is. But this doesn't mean you should have a large portion of your life savings in your company's stock.

After meeting with thousands of folks over the years, I've heard countless stories of how great each person's employer is, and why that person has a big chunk of their 401(k) tied up in its stock. There are many reasons for this. First, people are more familiar with their own employer than they are with any other company. Then there's the fact that management usually paints a bright future portrait of the company. Maybe the stock price is even discussed around the office on a regular basis. All that, and *you personally* have an interest in seeing the company succeed. You work there! You *want or even need* that company to thrive.

I own a company. Believe me, I understand.

But these are not great reasons to pick an investment. If you own some of your employer's stock within your

401(k), be honest with yourself: The only reason you own it is because you work there.

Now does *that* seem like a good-enough reason to hold so much of your future in one place? (It's actually a trick question as there is no good reason to lack diversification in your portfolio.)

It's never wise to overexpose yourself to one investment. Your employer already provides your paycheck, and your medical coverage, and maybe even a pension. Do you really want to increase your exposure to that one entity by putting your life savings there as well?

Of course not.

We all remember what happened at Enron. Okay, as you're reading this, you're thinking to yourself, "The company that I work for is not Enron." But do you realize that those employees who diversified their 401(k) account away from Enron minimized their losses? It's only those who had everything in Enron stock that lost their retirement savings. Others walked away from that mess with their 401(k)s almost totally intact.

So, a big part of good investment management is diversification. You'll want to remain diversified, not only as you transition into retirement, but beyond. Those who survived the tech bubble of the early 2000s, the real estate meltdown, and the financial crisis with their retirements intact did so because they were diversified.

Good diversification may not always yield the highest short-term returns. It's not glamorous. You can't brag about it. And it's not the lottery. But smart people empha-size diversification, because what it is designed to do is to reduce your risks and help insulate you from big events, and this provides you with a higher probability of a successful retirement.

Diversification protects you. And for a large majority of my more than 4,000 clients, it's a primary component of each investment portfolio that we create.

A **SOLID**
Approach

Poor investment management (or investment MIS-man-agement, as the case may be) is the single area that is most likely to derail your retirement. In respect to this, when it comes to investing, the two things you must know about yourself are your risk tolerance and your time horizon. Knowing your risk tolerance will help you avoid emotion-al investing (jumping in and out of the market), and this should, over time, keep you invested over the long haul, which should increase your odds of a successful transition to retirement. Knowing your specific time horizon allows you to choose investments that should have the most value at the point in the future when you need access to your savings.

Lastly, the two overarching investment principles that I encourage all my clients to adopt are, first, don't try and outsmart the markets and, second, get serious about portfolio diversification.

When it comes to timing the markets, even the experts are usually wrong. I recommend you take a consistent, long-view approach. Slow and steady wins the day. Second, a consistent approach works best when you are diversified. The people who survive market crashes, recessions, and black swan events with their investments and savings all (or mostly) intact are those people who are diversified.

RISK MANAGEMENT

IN THIS CHAPTER
YOU WILL LEARN...

- *How your risks evolve over time*

- *Risk management and NASA*

- *Lesser-known types of insurance*

Introduction

When I began writing *Personal Decision Points*, I repeatedly found myself looking ahead to this section. I was looking forward to it because not only is risk management perhaps the most overlooked aspect of retirement preparation, it's been my experience that very few people understand what it is.

Risk management is the process of identification, analysis, and either the acceptance or the mitigation of uncertainty in investment decision-making.

I wouldn't blame you if you were scratching your head.

Let's try a different approach.

A good place to begin might actually be with rockets. That's rockets as in the types launched by the National Aeronautics and Space Administration (NASA).

Think back a few decades.

Think about the sense of awe you felt while watching the first Space Shuttle launch or, for those a bit older, the Apollo rockets blasting off to the moon. There was a time when the most famous people on Earth were astronauts Buzz Aldrin and Neil Armstrong.

Walk on the moon, become a household name.

Now *that* makes perfect sense.

It makes sense because, when it came to expanding both the imagination *and the footprint* of mankind—even how we felt when we looked up into the sky—NASA changed our perception of what was possible. It makes sense because, not only had nothing close to this ever been done before, but because the entire mission was fraught with danger.

According to the Risk Management Page on the NASA website, do you know what one of the most important posts at NASA is? Risk management. That's because it involves, among other things, identifying and then preparing for things that have never happened before.

Risk management is the domain of the out-of-the-box thinkers. It's for people with keen powers of observation and anticipation, and only big brains need apply.

Getting Ready for the UNEXPECTED

While I wouldn't *precisely* equate retirement preparation with a lunar landing, key aspects of the process are similar. That's because it's your and your advisor's mission to identify risks, and then keep them at bay so you can travel through retirement with your finances intact.

"ALL COURSES OF ACTION ARE RISKY, SO PRUDENCE IS NOT IN AVOIDING DANGER (IT'S IMPOSSIBLE), BUT CALCULATING RISK AND ACTING DECISIVELY."

NICCOLO MACHIAVELLI,
THE PRINCE (1532)

Risk management can help make that happen.

Understandably, most of us don't like to spend too much time thinking about all the various things that could go wrong in our lives. But as you move into your retirement transition stage, it's crucial that some planning be undertaken that both *identifies* and *minimizes* the risks that could unnecessarily hurt you.

I'll cover the important topic of investment risk in a moment, but first I'd like to discuss risks that are mitigated (or eliminated) by insurance, along with a few risks that you probably never knew existed. This requires that we identify bigger-picture threats to your assets, such as living in a flood plain or straddling an earthquake fault, but also seemingly innocent decisions that could place your financial well-being in peril.

Your Risks
EVOLVE

As you age and move through life, your risks change and evolve. For example, when you are young and supporting a family, an early death would wreak financial havoc on your loved ones.

But that doesn't *have* to happen.

During the asset accumulation stage of life, the financial impact of the death of an income earner can be mitigated with the purchase of life insurance. But then that risk changes over time. Once the kids have grown, the fiscal impact of an early death may diminish and the need for life insurance can be reduced.

Later, you'll hopefully have accumulated enough money that you'll need the types of insurance that protect those assets.

Sounds easy enough.

But the fact is that not all risks are insurable. *Some* are circumstantial.

Here's a brief, but very common, example of a circumstantial risk that can only be avoided if it's identified. What you don't know can hurt you. Unfortunately, this particular scenario had serious consequences for a well-meaning person.

Here's what happens: A retiree changes their bank accounts, or even the title to their home, to have one of their children listed as a joint owner. The idea behind this is that it makes it easier for the child to help out with some of the bill paying while making it simpler to transfer assets after death.

What could be more straightforward?

Typically, listing a child as a joint owner is a mistake. For one thing, once a child is a joint owner to an account, that asset is subject to any creditors that the child may have, either now or in the future.

To repeat: You're trying to make things easier for your kid, but co-signing accounts places your assets at risk.

Think I'm exaggerating?

A close colleague of mine is an estate planning attorney whose client, an elderly widow, actually just lost her home to the IRS. This woman had always paid her bills and, in fact, didn't owe any back taxes whatsoever.

To help ease the transfer of her assets upon her death, she changed title to her savings, investments, and her home so that her oldest son was listed as a joint owner. This seemed to work fine for a number of years—that is, until the IRS got involved.

This well-intentioned woman's son, unbeknownst to her, believed that it was unconstitutional for the United States government to levy taxes. Because of this belief, he hadn't paid them for a number of years. When the IRS finally caught up with him, the agency went to collect the back taxes and seized everything he owned, which included the joint assets with his mother.

> **"HAVING A JOINT ACCOUNT WITH SOMEONE CAN RUIN YOU."**
>
> **SCOTT HANSON**

This may be a unique example, but this could have happened with any debt the son had, including random creditors, medical or dental bills, a divorce, or even a judgment if the son had lost a lawsuit. There's no going back, either. That's because even if the mother had taken her son off her accounts before the judgment, those creditors can still come calling and claim those assets.

INSURANCE NEEDS:
Definitions and Overview

Back to insurance risk management. Simply, what is it?

Insurance is a way for you to transfer your various *insurable risks* onto an insurance company. You're paying now in case you become deceased or incapacitated *later*. And you're paying now in case you make an innocent (or not so innocent) mistake, and some entity—be it the government or a private party—wants to be compensated for it.

Simply, insurance can protect you, your family, and your assets against outside claims. That's really all it does.

Insurance You
MIGHT Need

My business partner Pat McClain often says: "It's better to have it and not need it." He is, of course, 100 percent correct!

If you have accumulated money, savings, or investments, including owning a home (or you are in the process of accumulation), you need to take a sober, dispassionate look at what types of insurance you need.

Which is what we provide to our clients.

I want to emphasize that we don't sell insurance. But advising clients on what types of insurance they *might* need is an important part of the retirement transition process.

While everyone's situation is unique, here is an overview of *some* of the types of coverage that should be considered during retirement. I've intentionally left out descriptions of home and medical insurance to touch upon types of coverage that may be less familiar to many readers.

LIABILITY INSURANCE

As the name implies, liability insurance protects us against liability that we may have caused or been a party to. For example, if we inadvertently back into a car while pulling out of a parking space, we are liable for what it costs to repair any damages we've caused. If someone is on your property and gets hurt, it's very possible that you will be responsible for that person's injuries.

UMBRELLA INSURANCE

An umbrella policy is a type of insurance that covers those areas that may not be covered by your existing policies. As the name implies, it provides an umbrella of protection for all of your assets. What it really does, however, is to provide insurance *beyond* the limits of your car or home policies.

One of the many reasons that umbrella policies matter is that, in the event you are sued, you can actually be forced to pay from your *future* earnings. Not only do umbrella policies give you greater protection from lawsuits, they can also pay your legal fees or even the salary of someone you injure who has to miss work.

Umbrella insurance has three main advantages:

1. It gives buyers extra coverage against lawsuits.

2. It helps pay your legal defense, which could be $100,000 or more.

3. And it may provide coverage for some things not covered by your home or auto insurance (a boat or snowmobile you've rented, or a car accident in Europe).

QUICK TIP ABOUT UMBRELLA INSURANCE

Some people consider umbrella policies the best buy in all of insurance. It can cost as little as $200 for the first $1 million of insurance, and then around $100 for each $1 million after that.

LIFE INSURANCE

Life insurance is a protection against the loss of income if the insured passes away. When I was a child, I used to think that life insurance was something people purchased to somehow ease the pain of losing a loved one. In a sense, that's true. Because while no amount of money can take away the pain of losing the person or people you love, what life insurance actually does is cover the loss of income that a family or spouse or loved one would incur should an income earner pass away.

LONG-TERM CARE INSURANCE

Insurance that covers your stay for chronic health issues in a nursing home or hospice, along with home visits by a health professional, is long-term care insurance. Long-term care is concerned with the most intimate aspects of our existence: dressing, eating, mobility, and personal hygiene.

Long-term care insurance is expensive. There are several reasons for this, but one is that massive numbers of Baby Boomers are retiring every day, meaning there's been a huge increase in claims. Another reason is that modern medicine is keeping us alive longer, and a longer life means more healthcare costs. A third reason is that, as of late 2015, we are mired in an era of historically low interest rates, so the money paid to insurance companies (via premiums) that's being reinvested isn't getting anywhere near the returns of the past. A final reason long-term care is so expensive is a combination of the first three: Because it's become more difficult for insurance companies to turn a profit in the long-term care department, many companies have stopped selling it altogether. (Fewer insurers mean less competition, which equates to higher prices.)

LONG-TERM CARE
(70 percent of 65-year olds
will need long-term care)

QUICK TIP ABOUT LONG-TERM CARE INSURANCE

You're probably going to need it. According to the Department of Health and Human Services, 70 percent of the people who turned 65 in

2014 will need long-term care at some point in their lives. This means the odds that you (or a loved one) will require long-term care are a near certainty. But as you've just read, it's expensive and, just in case you are wondering, Medicare doesn't typically cover stays in nursing homes or, for that matter, most levels of in-home care.

Investment Risk
MANAGEMENT

Risk management is not only concerned with protecting yourself through various types of insurance and risk assessment, but through intelligently protecting yourself, your family, and your assets via investment diversification.

Discussed at length in Chapter 4, diversification is a core investment approach that reduces risk by allocating money among various financial instruments, industries, and categories. Diversification is a key strategy to help protect you against catastrophic events such as market crashes and black swan events. To achieve diversification, you should allocate your investments in such a way that they respond differently to various events or trends. For example, in a volatile market some of your investments may decline in value, while the value of others may actually rise or remain unchanged.

"I HAVE NOT BEEN THAT WISE. HEALTH I HAVE TAKEN FOR GRANTED. LOVE I HAVE DEMANDED, PERHAPS TOO MUCH AND TOO OFTEN. AS FOR MONEY, I HAVE ONLY REALIZED ITS TRUE WORTH WHEN I DIDN'T HAVE IT."

HEDY LAMARR

An **EXAMPLE**
of Diversification

Let's imagine that your entire portfolio is comprised of stock in companies that mine for, or transport, coal. You learn that all coal miners are going to go on strike and that the outlook for a quick resolution is not good. Your portfolio may take a nosedive. If, however, you've counterbalanced your coal-related stock with, say, stock in other utilities such as electrical power or oil, just a fraction of your portfolio will be impacted by the coal strike, while the gains in value of your other stocks *may* help offset the losses to your coal interests.

Naturally, this is a simplified example of what it means to be diversified. In actuality, you'd want to diversify even deeper so that all of your assets aren't dependent upon companies that could be negatively impacted by five straight years of moderate weather, but I assume you get the point.

Investment diversification is a key component of risk management. Additionally, you want to *not only* diversify by investing in different industries and sectors, but by seeking out different asset classes, such as real estate or stocks and bonds, which will all react differently to various events or trends.

The Risk of Being OVERLY Aggressive

While there are certainly many exceptions, people who are aggressive investors may be trying to realize greater returns by making riskier investments. Rather than emphasizing my preferred investment approach (asset preservation), some aggressive investors are less patient, like taking chances, and may need to have a strong tolerance for risk because their emphasis on the fast appreciation of capital may require their investments to receive near-constant oversight.

Some investors thrive on risk and actually enjoy the thrills associated with this type of approach. But for others, it's incredibly stressful. Just like individual investors, qualified advisors have strong opinions about what constitutes a sound investment strategy. The point is that I've seen too many volatile market eras to not understand that, when it comes to investing and retirement preparation, slow and steady is an approach that we believe works. Naturally, I always try to meet the needs of my clients, but my firm *typically* emphasizes asset preservation and long-view investing over the high-risk allocation of portfolios.

> "NEVER TEST THE DEPTH OF A RIVER WITH BOTH FEET."
>
> WARREN BUFFETT

Though, rest assured, I'm certainly not saying you should only invest in bonds or CDs. In fact, one key exception is that, while I always encourage my clients to emphasize a long-view approach, I do agree that younger investors can probably afford to be somewhat more aggressive with at least *some* of their allocations. (This is of course because younger investors have a longer time horizon before retirement.)

That said, I've seen it again and again: The markets are flying high, so emotional investors become more aggressive and begin to take more risks. But then comes the inevitable correction, the market falls, and those that jumped in are injured while the people who stepped lightly are understandably thrilled for having stayed the course and shown restraint. (This is called "availability bias," and it is a part of behavioral finance. Availability bias occurs when investors emphasize recent events, such as market surges, over history, because the recent events, like a bull market, are fresh in their minds.)

OVERSPENDING
Risk

The final risk I'd like to touch upon, and one that seems to hurt as many retirees as any other *manageable risk*, is that of overspending. When you transition into retirement and receive a lump-sum pension payout from your employer or cash out your 401(k), you may suddenly be in possession of hundreds of thousands, if not millions, of dollars which is likely more money than you've ever had in your life.

It seems like that kind of money will last forever (and it can). But all too often, it doesn't.

Think of all the horror stories about lottery winners and professional athletes. In spite of millions of dollars handed to them overnight, a large majority end up flat broke. These are not bad or weak people. They've simply never had any financial training or advice.

Comparatively, overspending risk is precisely what it seems: spending too much too early in retirement. It's particularly damaging because you're not only spending down the savings that you need to live on for the rest of your life, but it's money that you should be using to grow and enlarge your nest egg.

Budgets, qualified, professional investment advice and guidance, and proper asset allocation, along with an honest evaluation of your long-term goals and needs, go a long way toward remedying the threat of overspending.

Conclusion

Most of us don't want to think about what *might* go wrong in our lives. But when it comes to retirement, the advantage of being proactive is that you're more likely to take the necessary steps such as buying umbrella insurance, choosing to work with an advisor to help you identify risks, budget your finances, and allocate *and* maximize your savings.

What proper risk management does is to provide you with the opportunity to protect and prolong the life of your money, which should help you to enjoy your retirement to the fullest.

ESTATE AND LEGACY PLANNING

IN THIS CHAPTER
YOU WILL LEARN...

- *What a will does*

- *Who might need a living trust*

- *Why updating the beneficiaries on your retirement accounts is important*

Introduction

While this chapter is about estate and legacy planning, it could just as easily be about our fear of death or our propensity to procrastinate.

You'll understand why in a moment.

As with tax planning, right up front I want to make it very clear that I am not an estate planning attorney. The retirement transition process requires a team approach, and, along with a credentialed advisor and a qualified accountant, your team should also include an experienced, qualified, credentialed estate planning attorney.

Estate planning encompasses the tasks that serve to manage an individual's assets in the event of their incapacitation or death.

The term "estate" means something different to everyone. For many, when they hear that word they think of someone who has substantial wealth and lives in Malibu. But whether it's modest, or incredibly large and complex, we all have an estate. And we will all leave our estate to someone or something (perhaps a charity) when we die.

While estate plans are important, that doesn't mean they have to be complicated. What they do need to be is thoroughly thought-through, legally recorded, and documented.

NEVER Grow Old, NEVER Die

The purpose of an estate plan is to ensure that your wishes are met in the transfer of assets to your beneficiaries at the time of your death. Oftentimes, this can be accomplished with a simple will and proper documentation on retirement accounts (naming a beneficiary).

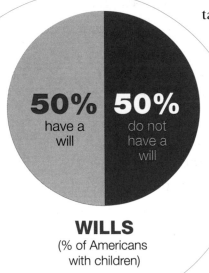

WILLS
(% of Americans with children)

But did you know that, according to a May 6th, 2012, article in *Forbes Magazine*, half of Americans with children don't even have a simple will? That's a problem, because even the estates of people with moderate wealth can *automatically* proceed to expensive and time-consuming probate if they die without one.

So if wills are so important, why do so many of us die without one?

Well, from my experience as a financial advisor for the past 25 years, there are two main reasons.

First, while we all generally accept that we are going to die, most of us don't believe that we are going to die today. This means that there's no real sense of urgency to do the estate planning because we think there's plenty of time.

Simply, we'll all just get around to doing it when we get a little older.

A second reason why we don't get around to having an estate plan put in place is we can't seem to decide how our assets should be distributed. And then even if we *can* decide, it may be that our spouse doesn't have the same opinion that we do and we can't come to a consensus.

Some people mistakenly believe that it's best to avoid uncomfortable conversations.

But an estate plan does not have to be perfect. Having a basic will is light years ahead of having nothing at all. So rather than waiting until you have the perfect strategy, it's best to get *something* in place as soon as possible. A will or trust can always be updated as your intentions change, and it has been my experience that just starting the process will move things along in a positive way.

"SETTING A GOAL IS NOT THE MAIN THING. IT IS DECIDING HOW YOU WILL GO ABOUT ACHIEVING IT AND STAYING WITH THAT PLAN."

TOM LANDRY

FACT-FINDING
Mission: Getting Your Assets in Order

Back to the process of deciding what goes where. First, gather your facts.

When you think about what kind of legacy you are going to leave, no matter how large or small, whether it's to your family or to causes that you hold dear, start by taking a look at what makes up your material life. It's always a good idea to put together an inventory worksheet to catalog your real estate, business interests, financial investments, retirement accounts, and other savings. List your cash, bank accounts, and retirement accounts, and make sure to include future interests such as trusts, insurance policies, funds, or properties or inheritance you expect to receive at a later date.

Once you have a complete inventory, it's important to understand the nature of these assets, and how they can be handled in your estate, along with any legal restrictions your assets may be subject to.

This includes the kinds of taxes each asset may incur.

With thoughtful planning, it's possible to maximize your estate to the letter of the law while simultaneously working to minimize taxes on particular assets, such as cash and bank accounts.

This takes *pre-planning* and preparation, and this can save your heirs a lot of money.

Next, anticipate *your* long-term needs, as well as the long-term needs of your spouse or partner and dependents. Do you have minor children or family members with special needs or circumstances? According to the March of Dimes, 22 percent of families have a special needs child. If you are one of the 22 percent, you will want to choose a guardian.

Our Own
Special Needs and
LIVING TRUSTS

The first steps of a well-thought-out legacy plan may include deciding between setting up a last will and testament or setting up a living trust. Unlike a will, a living trust is not a document; rather, it's a method of protecting and managing properties to ensure that the intended parties maintain control of the assets.

A living trust is when a trustee holds the legal possession of a fund or assets that belong to another person (the beneficiary), and is created while the person is still alive. In other words, you intentionally transfer title to your property from your name to that of the trustee. This allows you to place your property under the supervision of one entity so that your property can be more efficiently distributed when you die.

One of the biggest advantages of a living trust is that, while it generally costs more, it is not subject (as wills are) to expensive and time-consuming probate (more on this later).

What Is **A WILL** and Who Needs One?

A will is a signed and witnessed written document that outlines how you wish to distribute your assets upon your death.

I recently received a call to our financial topic radio program, *Hanson McClain's Money Matters*, from a man in his late 60s who is retired. He had just attended a seminar on living trusts with his wife. He wanted to know if they really needed a will. Then he informed me that they had just about all of their assets in IRAs valued at about $1.5 million (with designated beneficiaries), along with two homes in California valued at $400,000 and $500,000.

My answer: *Emphatically yes!*

Here's the thing: When you set up a living trust, you do some estate planning where you have a will that will indicate how your assets should be distributed, as well as some other documents that provide power of attorney in the event something should happen to you (such as mental incapacitation). Usually retirement accounts (IRAs and 401(k)s, for instance) will pass on to your designated beneficiaries regardless of what you state in your trust (make sure these are up-to-date), but property is treated as something else entirely.

There's more: The gentleman above also told me that he had no kids, and that most of their money would go to an education fund for their grandnieces and grandnephews.

Make no mistake, they still need a trust. And even more so, because as they have no children, they may need it to ensure that no one can contest it.

But here's something to consider. If you are in a similar situation—that is, you have no children or immediate family to designate as your beneficiaries—you can get a leg up by working with the charity that you wish to support. Even if you have children, if you want to give, say, 10 percent or more of your assets to a charity, that charity will probably pay to set up the trust. Keep in mind that in this situation, it's actually better to leave some of the $1.5 million in the IRAs (versus leaving the real estate) to the charity. That's because a charity doesn't pay any income taxes. If you leave that IRA to nieces or nephews, they'll have to pay taxes on it.

In the case of our client, I encouraged him and his wife to have some fun and make a list of separate charities they care about, and then come together and compare their notes and really think about ways to leave lasting legacies.

And in the end? That's exactly what they did! They were able to designate funds for their nieces and nephews *as well as* their beloved nonprofits.

Remember, envisioning the legacy you'll leave behind *not only* makes you feel good, it can help you sleep better at night.

A couple of tips:

- Formulate an estate plan with your partner.
- Have a series of family discussions to set expectations.
- Gather a team of experts (investment advisor, attorney, accountant, insurance agent) to protect you and to help make the decisions that will best suit your desires, as well as to help you meet the needs of those you leave behind.

It's not a pleasant thought, but the hard truth is that dying is not free. As we work with our clients to do estate planning, we also have to take the cost of death itself into consideration. What kind of funeral and burial or death arrangements do you want? Make certain you designate funds and directives in the amounts and to the degrees that you'll need to cover these costs.

Lessen the Expense of **PROBATE** with Foresight and Planning

When you die, your assets essentially fall into two categories: those that avoid probate, and those that require probate. Anything that you have in your physical possession, such as artwork, clothing, jewelry, heirlooms, furnishings, vehicles, entertainment equipment, and other personal property and possessions, do not require probate.

Those assets which you do *not* have in your physical possession, such as bank accounts, stocks, credit union accounts, insurance policies, mutual funds, annuities, bonds, certificates of deposit, as well as real estate, are all subject to probate—unless you have named beneficiaries on the title.

Generally, your heirs will have to pay taxes on inheritances.

From a tax standpoint, certain assets—mutual funds, stocks, a piece of real estate—get stepped up to fair market value on the day you die. So, keep in mind that whatever gain has occurred during your lifetime, when you pass away and leave that asset to an heir, the person who inherits it gets it at the fair market value.

> **"IN THIS WORLD NOTHING CAN BE SAID TO BE CERTAIN, EXCEPT DEATH AND TAXES."**
>
> **BENJAMIN FRANKLIN**

And the current fair market value is how it will be taxed.

To repeat: Dying can be expensive! Probate taxes, if assets are not properly safeguarded, can be painfully high (and the process is time-consuming).

Tax on an inherited IRA can be anywhere from zero to 39.6 percent!

But if you pass along your property in the form of a will or trust, you can usually avoid probate. If you die intestate (without a will), for example, and you have assets upwards of $25,000 (although this varies by state), your estate will have to go through probate.

The probate process essentially involves the court gathering your assets, holding on to them for a while, and then distributing them among your creditors and inheritors.

The general steps include:

- Your designated executor (someone assigned by the state if you have no will) files appropriate papers with the court.
- The court accounts for your assets and property.
- The court notifies any beneficiaries and creditors of your death.
- The court pays your outstanding debts (including taxes).
- The court distributes your assets.

The probate process is lengthy and costly. By contrast, the costs of setting up a living trust are not only less—but they also can safeguard your assets, mitigate hefty taxes, and get the property quickly into the hands of those you intended, all of which should give you serious peace of mind.

When it comes to selecting between a will or a living trust, the best strategy depends upon your unique situation—be sure to investigate the pros and cons of each. A trust may provide the control you prefer, but you *may* feel the setup costs and management expense are not worth your time and money.

As a reminder: It's important to remember that both wills and trusts are subject to taxes.

A Common (AND COSTLY) Mistake

It's amazing how many of us think that we have our estate plan in order, yet have still overlooked a very simple thing: making certain that the beneficiaries on our retirement accounts and life insurance policies are up-to-date.

This could well be the most important part of this chapter.

- **WHEN YOU PASS AWAY, YOUR RETIREMENT ACCOUNTS (IRAS, 401(K)S, 403(B)S, 457S, ETC.) WILL BE TRANSFERRED TO THE LISTED BENEFICIARIES, REGARDLESS OF WHAT YOUR WILL STATES.**

That's right! *The beneficiaries listed on your retirement accounts supersede those listed in your will.*

So, if your will states that your IRA should go to your two children, but you still have your ex-spouse listed on the beneficiary form you filled out years ago, your IRA will actually go to your ex.

I've seen it happen numerous times, and it's tragic.

Again, it is vitally important to keep beneficiary forms on retirement accounts and life insurance policies up-to-date.

Special Situations Require **PERIODIC STATUS CHECKS**

You may be a savvy, thoughtful planner who has already set up an estate plan, and you may think you can now sit back and think, "Ah! Sweet retirement, I've got all my ducks in a row."

But the reality is, life is ever-changing and we continue to find our family members and ourselves in new circumstances.

Any time you go through a life change or event of some kind, it's the perfect opportunity to take inventory of your assets and reevaluate your legacy plan.

When should you reevaluate?

- You've lost your spouse.

- You've gotten married or remarried.

- You've gained a child, stepchild or grandchild.

- You've gotten divorced.

- A beneficiary has died.

If you're married and living in California (and a few other states), any assets that you generate during the marriage are community property, 50/50. Any assets that you had *prior* to your marriage are considered separate property. Now, depending on how you structure things during your marriage, those assets you had before your marriage may remain separate property, or they may be comingled and become community property.

Whether because of happy events or unfortunate hardships, circumstances change. It's easy to forget that a 401(k) or a will you've had for 20 years still has your ex-husband listed as the beneficiary.

But neglect can hurt the people we love.

You may know someone who doesn't speak to a formerly close family member over hard feelings that were completely avoidable had the proper planning just been undertaken. I've seen it dozens of times. And so I implore you, as one of the key lessons of *Personal Decision Points*, if you love your family, become determined NOT to leave this world without taking care to avoid the heartache that results from dying without a carefully considered will, or without updating your beneficiaries on your insurance and your retirement accounts.

Safeguard Your
VIRTUAL LIFE
and Digital Estate

Ah, the considerations of modern life!

We live in a digital world, and in that realm, our lives continue on after we die. When thinking about your estate, you may neglect to consider online bank accounts, invest-ment accounts, email archives, and profiles on LinkedIn, Facebook, Instagram, and the like. But our online life needs protecting and planning ahead for the transferring, closing, or safeguarding of our intellectual and financial property and our private digital footprint.

Leaving these things intact, as though it doesn't matter because you are gone, actually sets you up for identity theft because there's no one watching the store.

Think I'm exaggerating? "The deceased are vulnerable to identity theft because the family is in mourning and they're not paying attention to the deceased person's fi-nances or personal information," says Sonya Smith-Valen-tine, an attorney who specializes in identity theft.

It's a lot of work to clear up identity theft, and it's be-yond inconvenient for your spouse or heirs to have to prove to a credit card company that you've been deceased for six months and couldn't possibly have purchased a diamond necklace in Monaco.

Make a list of your digital assets, along with all your passwords, and include these among your important docu-ments. Include information about what you want to have done with your accounts and whom you designate to han-dle them after you die. Do you have a complete list of pass-words and profiles for your online accounts in a safe place? Does your spouse or partner or designated executor know where to find this information in the event of an emer-gency (or your passing)?

Identity theft of the recently deceased is a huge and growing problem. Deal with it in advance, and save your loved ones from this misery.

Making Your **LIST** and Checking It Twice

Once you've made your legacy plan, sit back and review your choices. Take the time to make sure you know the answers to these questions:

- Who is your power of attorney assigned to?
- Do you have a living will or healthcare directive?
- What is your plan to protect your minor children?
- What is your plan to take care of your spouse?
- Have you chosen an executor wisely?
- Are your documents current, reflecting your new or recent lifestyle changes?
- Are your documents in a safe place?
- Are your passwords, driver's license, and Social Security number where your heirs can find them?
- Do you understand the gift tax and estate tax laws where you live?
- Have you looked for tax loopholes?

Unfortunately, even the best legacy plans can still meet with conflict and be contested by family members. It's a sad but common occurrence when people die. But the more thoughtful planning we can put into it now, the better. It may mean choosing to transfer assets to beneficiaries while you're still alive, or determining ways to protect inherited funds from your children's potential conflicts, but that is life and avoiding these considerations won't make these problems go away.

Ultimately you want to ensure that your wishes will be carried out, and that you can protect your assets for your surviving spouse, family members, organizations, or causes. Remember, some estate planning is better than no planning at all. Having *something* in place is the best first step. It's okay if it's not perfect—you can always improve it along the way.

It's your legacy—plan to keep it that way.

DISTRIBUTION AND INCOME SOURCES

IN THIS CHAPTER
YOU WILL LEARN...

- *Why the order in which you draw down your retirement accounts matters*

- *How divorce impacts Social Security*

- *Common mistakes that can cost you thousands of dollars*

Introduction

When it comes time to plan for retirement, figuring out which investment and retirement accounts are the best sources from which to derive your income—and in what sequence—can be a tricky process.

Make no mistake, the source and sequencing matters.

When I present this topic to clients, it's not unusual for them to have never considered it before. But a creative, well-thought-out strategy for choosing your distribution and income sources can reduce your tax burden and save you money.

As detailed throughout *Personal Decision Points*, it's my hope that you've gained an understanding of what retirement transition is. Simply, by now you know it's not an investment strategy.

The next step is to figure out which accounts should be set up for distributions and which assets should be held in reserve.

Ideally, when you are transitioning, you have several sources from which to draw income. You may have an IRA or two. You probably have an employer-sponsored retirement plan, such as a 401(k) or 403(b). Maybe you're one of the fortunate few who still has an employer pension. You might have some after-tax monies in a brokerage account or in mutual funds. Plus, at some point, you'll probably have Social Security to tap in to (though I'm more than a little concerned about the state of that retirement program).

You've worked your entire life saving and preparing for retirement, and while Chapter 1: Retirement Income Needs, emphasizes the importance of finding ways to live off the income from your investments, the reality is that not everyone will be able to do that. If that's you, then comes the time when you have to consider how to draw down your principal. Determining which accounts to take distributions from, how much to take, which ones to defer, and so on, are not one-time processes. The reality is that they are ongoing, and fluid, and mistakes can cost you dearly.

Simply put, if you have two or more of the income sources mentioned above, *how* and *when* you go about taking your distributions will matter to you and impact your financial health, in both the short and long term.

A Common **INCOME DISTRIBUTION SCENARIO** That Could Cost You Thousands

A few years back a couple came to our firm for some retirement advice. They had been out of the workforce for a number of years and had never before met with a financial advisor.

These folks were a fairly typical middle-class couple with a home, a small pension, Social Security, a large IRA rollover, and some money in a brokerage account. The brokerage account consisted of a small amount of cash, a few stocks, and a couple of mutual funds.

To keep taxes to a minimum, this couple had been drawing from their brokerage account and had let the IRA rollover continue to grow. This had worked well as far as reducing their *current* tax obligations, but it was setting them up for a big sting at age 70½.

They had no idea what was coming.

Because a good portion of their income had come from drawing down cash in their brokerage account, their taxable income was very low each year. (This put them in the 15 percent bracket.)

The problem that was lurking around the corner was the IRS's required minimum distributions from the IRA once the husband reached age 70½. (The amount that is required

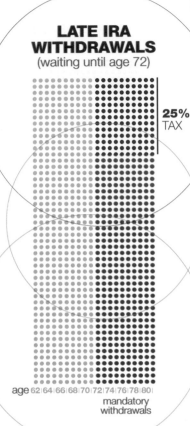

LATE IRA WITHDRAWALS
(waiting until age 72)

25%
TAX

age 62|64|66|68|70|72|74|76|78|80|
mandatory
withdrawals

is determined by a formula set by the IRS, which starts at just under 4 percent annually and rises each year.)

Based upon the large balance in this gentleman's IRA, it was obvious that he was going to have required minimum distributions in excess of $50,000 in just three years. This would push their taxable income well into the 25 percent federal tax bracket and needlessly cost them thousands of dollars.

The tremendous mistake this couple made the past several years was to not take advantage of IRA distributions while they were in the 15 percent tax bracket. Using some calculations from their tax return, I quickly realized that they could have withdrawn an additional $20,000 in income.

Because this couple was unaware of their options, they were faced with a tax increase of over 66 percent. That's right. They could have paid taxes at a 15 percent federal rate, but would soon be hit with a tax rate of 25 percent.

Again, it's all about preparation, information and planning.

How did this happen? They thought that they were doing the right thing because they had heard, from more than one source, that you should defer your IRA for as long as possible. While this may be true for some folks, every situation is unique and this was clearly not the best thing for these two.

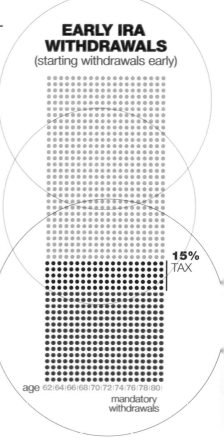

EARLY IRA WITHDRAWALS
(starting withdrawals early)

15% TAX

age 62|64|66|68|70|72|74|76|78|80|
mandatory
withdrawals

Had they been working with a good financial advisor as they transitioned into retirement, they would have either taken IRA distributions of roughly $20,000 per year or, better still, they would have converted $20,000 per year from his IRA to a Roth IRA. This would have enabled them to "lock in" the tax rate at 15 percent rather than defer their entire IRA account only to pay taxes at 25 percent later on.

IRAs, 401(k)s, and Other QUALIFIED RETIREMENT ACCOUNTS

It's pretty simple: Don't automatically defer your retirement accounts. For your working career, you've probably focused on deferring as much income as possible. I'm all for it! Now that you are moving into retirement, it's time to start planning how those dollars will be distributed. Deferring retirement accounts until age 70½ might make sense for some, but for many, it's probably best to distribute some income before the IRS demands it.

Distributions from most retirement accounts are all taxed the same—the money withdrawn is taxed as ordinary income. However, there are a couple of important exceptions.

First, some older 401(k) plans may have an accumulation of "after-tax" dollars. These are monies that have been contributed that were in excess of the annual limits, so while they were able to go into the 401(k), they did not receive a tax deduction.

When a 401(k) is distributed upon retirement, because these deposits were after-tax dollars, these funds can be withdrawn without incurring any taxes.

Another exception is where a 401(k), ESOP, or other profit-sharing plan has employer stock as a position. In this event, the stock can be distributed and taxed as ordinary income only on the cost basis—what you paid for the stock. All the gains are deferred and will be taxed as long-term capital gains when sold in the future.

As introduced in Chapter 3: Tax Planning, this strategy is known as net unrealized appreciation (NUA).

Keep in mind that NUA only works if you own actual company shares within your employer's retirement plan and have those shares distributed to you, not rolled into an IRA. Once you move the shares into an IRA (or other retirement plan), you are precluded from utilizing the favorable NUA tax treatment.

It's also worth mentioning that money from your employer's retirement plan can be received *prior* to age 59½ without any tax penalties, provided you were age 55 (or older) in the year in which you left your job. So, if you retire early at, say, age 57, you can receive money from your employer's plan without being hit with an early withdrawal penalty. But once you move these funds into an IRA, they are tied up until age 59½.

There is also a way of receiving retirement distributions from IRAs (and other qualified retirement plans) prior to age 59½ without any tax penalties. As long as you establish a distribution that is designed to last you until your dying day, and you follow all of the restrictions under IRC 72(t), you can actually receive retirement income without triggering early withdrawal penalties.

We spoke with one 70-year-old woman who has a traditional IRA with a large institution, a 403(b), and a small credit union IRA valued at $6,000 paying 1.5 percent interest (and which wouldn't mature for a few years).

Her other funds added up to $584,000.

She wanted to know how to take the minimum distribution from the IRA without breaking it.

First of all, nearly every financial product allows for required minimum distributions. In the case of our client, it comes down to some basic calculation. Add the two IRAs together, figure out what the required minimum distributions are, and just take it from the IRA. As soon as it matures, take the $6,000 and put it in with the $584,000 dollars. Move the 403(b) in the IRA as well.

Your goal should be to simplify your life by putting all the funds into one account. That's because there's no real benefit to keeping the money in three different places (unless it's some old, locked-in contract that's getting a higher interest rate than we're seeing elsewhere at this time).

Once you reach age 59½, you may take distributions from your IRA without penalty. Remember, your IRA funds are pre-taxed income (meaning you will be required to pay taxes on those distributions). However, depending on your needs, you can allocate those distributions to be paid out monthly or annually.

AFTER-TAX Savings

There are a number of different ways to think about the money you've accumulated in your savings and money market accounts. Some people feel the need to keep a large amount set aside in cash "just in case." (It's always a good idea to have some cash available in the event of an emergency or unforeseen event.)

You might find yourself in a situation where your pension, Social Security, and IRA withdrawals provide the majority of your income, but still find that you need a little extra money from time to time. If you were to tap into your IRA or 401(k), you'd have the taxman to contend with, and it could cost you a third of your withdrawal. So, in situations like this, tapping into your cash savings may be the way to go.

Or, if you are in a position where you have a large amount in after-tax savings as well as other non-IRA assets, such as stocks or mutual funds, drawing down your after-tax savings may be the best solution for both short-term as well as long-term tax planning.

SECURITIES Outside of Retirement Accounts

Money invested in mutual funds, stocks, bonds, etc., that are held outside of retirement accounts can be a great source of income. With these holdings, you get to control the timing of your taxation based upon when you decide to sell something and trigger a capital gain.

The capital gains tax rates are progressive, just like income tax rates, but the maximum federal rate is 20 percent (for most assets) versus 39.6 percent for ordinary income such as IRA withdrawals.

For many of our retired clients, we hold all of their securities in a single brokerage account. This not only makes things simple at tax time, but it also provides a mechanism for monthly income.

Most mutual funds pay some sort of dividend, typically quarterly, as well as a year-end capital gains distribution. Dividend-paying stocks provide income on a quarterly basis, while bonds provide income semiannually.

By having all of your securities in one account, you can establish a monthly income that can be deposited into your checking account. This provides an easy way to budget your income without having to worry about changing dividend amounts.

Social SECURITY

By now, you've surely read my concerns regarding the state of Social Security. Let's face it: There's a tidal wave of retirees entering the system and too few people paying into the program for it to survive in its present state. I do believe that Social Security will survive (I believe almost anything is possible), but I also believe that over the next 20 years the changes to the program will be more substantial than anything we've seen to date.

Here's the key: *When* you elect to take Social Security benefits is important. Why?

The fact is that when the time comes to collect Social Security, the right strategy can be worth thousands of dollars to you over the duration of your retirement. The best way to maximize your benefits depends on your age, your marital status, whether you're widowed, how much money you earned during your working years (and over what duration of time), your current financial status, and a host of other considerations. Obviously, there is no one-size-fits-all strategy. That's why it's especially important to become educated about the various options so that you can make the decision that is right for you and your family.

> **"THE QUESTION ISN'T AT WHAT AGE I WANT TO RETIRE, IT'S AT WHAT INCOME."**
>
> **GEORGE FOREMAN**

Ultimately, there are a couple ways to go: You can choose to claim Social Security benefits early, and let your other retirement assets grow. Or you can defer Social Security, thereby receiving a larger monthly amount when you do apply, and for the time being live off your other assets.

Regardless of your portfolio, your prime objective is to make informed decisions about how you accrue your benefits and when you elect to collect them. The age at which you apply for Social Security greatly affects your monthly allowance (the amount you receive). You may begin to draw benefits at age 62; however, if you are in a position where you can rely on other assets to draw

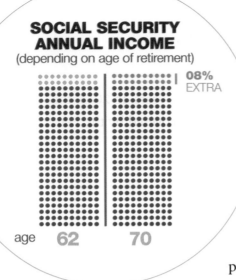

SOCIAL SECURITY ANNUAL INCOME
(depending on age of retirement)

08% EXTRA

age **62** **70**

from during your retirement years, it can pay to wait before you claim Social Security.

The difference between a monthly allowance at 62 versus one that you would receive if you wait until age 70 can add up to an additional 8 percent a year, plus interest.

Social Security and **DIVORCE**

If you are divorced, depending on how long you were married, and depending on whether or not you're remarried (and how long you waited to remarry), you may be eligible to collect spousal benefits because of your ex (and they never need to know). This is true of survivor benefits as well (if you outlive your spouse or ex). Keep in mind that if you file for your benefits and spousal or survivor benefits at the same time, you can only collect on one. In this case, working with a credentialed advisor to determine which will pay you more in the short term, and the long term, can help you decide which is the best option for your unique situation.

Company **PENSION**

The results are in: Company pensions have been on the decline in the United States for the past thirty-plus years. In 2015, the total number of defined benefit plans as covered by the Pension Benefit Guarantee Corporation's single-employee insurance program is at a historic low of 22,697. More and more, companies are reaching out to their beneficiaries and offering a single payout in lieu of continuing monthly payments. Take the case of one 69-year-old who was drawing $750 per month on his pension and received an offer for a one-time payment of $109,000. His other assets totaled about $1.3 million, and he was drawing about $5,000 a month from those. Now, if he took the $109,000 and put it into an account, at the end of normal remaining life expectancy of 17.8 years, he'd need about a 4½ percent return in order to earn the same amounts as he'd get by taking $750 a month for 17.8 years. In this case, it makes sense for him to take the lump sum and roll it into an IRA and start taking distributions of $750 per month.

However, if that pension was the only money he had in the world, I would advise him to keep it.

When it comes to determining whether you want to take your pension as a lump sum, in a single payout, or as an annuity (a lifetime monthly income), take the time to look at your big asset picture. If you choose the annuity route, you may opt between a **single-life annuity** and a **joint-and-survivor annuity**. The advantage of a single-life annuity is that it will pay you the largest monthly sum during the course of your life—until the day you die. That's fine if you are single. But if you are married, your spouse will be left high and dry, so the wiser choice is the joint-and-survivor annuity. With this type of benefit, you generally have the choice among a 100, 75, or 50 percent option. The 100 percent annuity provides your surviving spouse or other named beneficiary the same monthly benefits that you received; the 75 percent option provides three-quarters of what your monthly earnings were, and the 50 percent option pays out half of what you earned. You'll receive the highest monthly payments with the 50 percent option, and the lowest with the 100 percent option.

OTHER Assets

Other assets you may have saved, perhaps in the form of rental real estate or business ventures, obviously need to be taken into consideration when mapping out your retirement distribution sources. As you approach retirement, or perhaps as you are reevaluating your financial needs during the course of your retirement years, it's a good time to take stock in what you have outside of normal distribution income sources to make sure you're getting the most bang for your buck.

Do you have rental property or other real estate that is still working for you? Or are you finding that maintenance and upkeep or depreciation values are hitting you harder than the value of what you have? It may mean thinking about ways to turn those properties into a new investment, or looking at ways to transfer your properties to your beneficiaries while you are living in order to mitigate estate and death taxes that could affect your surviving spouse, children, and other beneficiaries.

You may be of the mindset of never really retiring, and keeping your foot in various business ventures. This could be an ideal way to keep some liquidity options at your fingertips while you're enjoying a time of working less or earning less than you did during your working years.

If you do consider re-entering the work arena after retirement, say in a part-time fashion, think about ways that you can make it work best for you. For example, if once upon a time you worked for an employer that offered a pension plan, you may be able to work part-time for that same employer and then continue to earn pension benefits even on a part-time basis.

There are, obviously, a lot of choices and decisions that must be made.

Live Necessarily **LONG**, Not Necessarily Large

If you're one of the lucky individuals who has accumulated a considerable amount of savings and assets earlier than most of your peers—say, thanks to good timing with investments, savings rates, or stock options—you might think, "Ah! Why not retire early?" And you may well just do that.

But if you haven't taken the time to really assess the impact of a longer retirement, you may be in for a surprise. Those first long years might seem more like a permanent vacation, living a life of leisure that includes more golf, dining out, traveling, and all sorts of entertainment activities, but all of these revolve around spending money.

> ## "IF YOU BUY THINGS YOU DO NOT NEED, SOON YOU WILL HAVE TO SELL THINGS YOU NEED."
>
> ### WARREN BUFFETT

Perhaps in the back of your mind you think, "Oh, I can always return to work, so I can up my earning power if I need to." The truth is, we can't assume that those options will actually be there for us if and when we need them, nor can we be sure that our desire or ability to work will be there if the opportunity is available.

If you are indeed fortunate enough to have access to rich resources in your retirement years, you essentially can do one of two things: Use those resources up, or make them work for you and turn them into wealth.

When it comes to your distribution and income sources during retirement, remember, you can always reevaluate, reassess, and restructure your plan. No matter your situation, for maximum results, there are always basic tenets to keep in mind:

- Decrease waste; increase efficiency
  - Are your money flow options at the lowest fee and taxable rates possible?
  - Are your income and growth assets performing?
  - Are there areas in your day-to-day life where you can downsize expenses without downsizing quality of life?
  - Are there areas for improvement?
- Turn savings into growth
  - Once you've trimmed some fat, turn those savings around and invest in areas that will help you increase your revenue streams.
- Indulge in meaningful activities
  - Having extra time on our hands in retirement can come with unexpected difficulties—no matter how much we've been looking forward to kicking back and living the good life. But when you invest your time in ways that give you joy—whether it's perfecting your golf swing or volunteering in your community—you may be delightfully surprised to find that it opens unexpected doors to living leaner, longer, and financially stronger.

Whatever your situation, be sure that you are not living beyond your means. We met a man who at 78 was spending

$4,500 a month out of his total assets of $350,000. He was unmarried, living in a retirement community, and pulling a monthly draw of a relatively high distribution—about 15 percent. As a straight-line distribution (say it's in bank CDs earning about 1 percent) that money is not going to last eight full years. We had to be frank with him: he was living in a more expensive community than he could afford. It's a terrible conversation to have, but this was the danger: In just eight years, he would be at zero, having drained his assets dry. In this case, we work backwards and start asking, what happens if you live 15 years versus eight years, or 20 years—what does that look like? In this man's case, he was 80 percent blind and had no way of getting around. In addition to looking for more affordable living, he would be wise to reach out to social services to locate a senior advocate who could help him determine whether he qualifies for special resources that may be available in the city, county, or state where he lives.

"SOONER OR LATER I'M GOING TO DIE, BUT I'M NOT GOING TO RETIRE."

MARGARET MEAD

If you think you're in a situation like that and your financial advisor has not been up front with you, that's the time to get a new financial advisor.

A gentleman of 85 came to us who had been drawing income solely from his Social Security and IRA, and for the first time he was planning on drawing money from a couple of portfolios. One was strictly for dividend income (preferred stocks, exchange-traded funds, secured debts, core stocks), producing at 6 percent. The other portfolio was strictly for growth, with an outlook of 14 percent over five years. His intention was to draw just income from the dividend portfolio, and draw on only the gain on the growth portfolio (provided there was any gain).

Our bigger question for him was what provisions had he made for his spouse to continue with retirement once he passed on? The income portfolio is only a percentage of the draw that he and his wife needed; if he plans to take the remainder only from his growth income, what happens in the down years?

If there's no growth, there's no income. So it's feast or famine.

In cases like this, what you want to do is set up a withdraw strategy to come up with something consistent, and then set aside another pot to grow.

The main thing is that you go out and get a financial advisor that you trust to help you create the best strategy for your situation.

Take the
BIG-PICTURE View

When it comes to your distribution and income sources, it's important to think about which assets you should have in your retirement plan, and which assets you should exclude. If, for example, you have $100,000 in your IRA and $100,000 in a brokerage account, it's only human nature to want to compare those accounts. But this is the challenge I give you: Step back and view these portfolios as one.

Here's what I'm talking about: Think about the benefits the government gives you now on capital gains versus ordinary income, and how that taxation works on retirement accounts and qualified dividends. Everything that comes out of your retirement plan will be taxed as ordinary income, regardless of how that income was derived inside that account. Everything that comes as interest from a bond will be taxed as ordinary income. So we know those two will be taxed as ordinary income.

Now, let's say you have a diversified portfolio, such as some S&P 500 index funds, and you have that fund outside of a retirement plan. That will grow somewhat tax-efficiently because it will have mostly capital appreciation, some dividends, and a little bit of capital gains distribution. It will also have capital gains tax treatment down the road, which are taxed favorably as qualified.

So, consider those assets that have favorable tax treatment today, such as real estate and stock index funds, as compared to bonds and retirement plans, which are taxed as ordinary income.

All things being equal, you generally want to have your fixed income inside your retirement account (your bond portion of the portfolio) and your equities—those growth things—outside your retirement account, and manage those assets tax-efficiently.

Let's say you're retired today, and you're pulling a certain amount of income from your retirement account and a certain amount from other assets. At Hanson McClain, we'd take that into consideration because you don't want to be forced to sell stocks or real estate in a down market; likewise, you don't want to be forced to take more out of your retirement account and have that taxed as ordinary income.

Obviously, as we near retirement, careful planning needs to be emphasized.

If you take the big-picture view and look at your entire portfolio as one entity, ideally you want those high-income-producing investments inside the retirement account, and the high capital gains producing assets outside the retirement account.

That's why it makes a lot of difference what assets you hold where. And that's why you need an advisor that you trust who can guide you through the ever-changing and complex financial landscape that faces everyone as they transition into retirement.

In Closing

While preparing for the future is something that most of us think about, far too many of us hesitate to begin the process in earnest until we are confronted with sometimes difficult choices or less-than-ideal circumstances. But as with any important endeavor, the longer you wait, the more difficult a seamless retirement transition becomes. The people who live well throughout their retirements typically do so because they took the initiative to work with experts to create a comprehensive plan.

The *7 Personal Decision Points* of the retirement transition process have been developed by myself and Hanson McClain Advisors' co-Founder and principal Pat McClain, as a way to familiarize you with the foundational aspects of a comprehensive approach to the retirement transition process.

We hope you found it informative and rewarding.

SCOTT T. HANSON,
CFP®, CFS®, CHFC
FINANCIAL ADVISOR

Scott Hanson is a senior partner and founding principal of Hanson McClain. A nationally recognized financial expert, he has been named to *Barron's* list of the Top 100 Independent Wealth Advisors in America for 2011, 2012, 2013, 2014 and 2015, and has been listed as one of the 25 most influential people in the financial services industry nationwide. Scott has been a guest on numerous television outlets including ABC News, CNBC, Fox and others, and has provided commentary for a variety of print and digital outlets, including *Kiplinger*, *CNBC.com*, *The Wall Street Journal*, *The New York Times*, and the *Los Angeles Times*.

For over 20 years, Scott has co-hosted Money Matters, a call-in, financial topic radio program that airs every weekend on flagship AM stations in Sacramento, San Francisco, Los Angeles, San Diego and Denver, and is available via podcast at MoneyMatters.com.

The 2011 winner of the Salvation Army's Spirit of Caring Award, Scott is a CERTIFIED FINANCIAL PLANNER™ practitioner, and has also earned the professional designations of Certified Fund Specialist (CFS®) and Chartered Financial Consultant (ChFC).

A SPECIAL
THANK YOU TO
SEAN HARVEY &
**IRISH CANON
PRESS**,
WITHOUT WHOM
THIS BOOK WOULD
NOT HAVE BEEN
POSSIBLE.